Do Brilliantly
AS European History

Derrick Murphy

Series Editor: Jayne de Courcy

Contents

Published by HarperCollins*Publishers*
77–85 Fulham Palace Road
London W6 8JB

www.**Collins**Education.con
On-line support for schools and colleges

First published 2002

ISBN 0 00 712605 0

British Library Cataloguing in Publication Data
A catalogue record for this book is available from the British Library

Edited by Steve Attmore
Production by Kathryn Botterill
Design by Gecko Ltd
Cover design by Susi Martin-Taylor
Printed and bound by Scotprint, Haddington

466165

Acknowledgements
The Author and Publishers are grateful to the following for permission to reproduce copyright material:

AQA Specimen examination questions (pp. 7, 23–24, 28–31, 34, 41, 46, 47, 52, 57, 63 and 65) are reproduced by permission of the Assessment and Qualifications Alliance.

Edexcel Specimen examination questions (pp. 12, 25, 36–38, 44–45, 49, 54–55 and 59–61) are reproduced by permission of Edexcel.

OCR Specimen examination questions (pp. 16–17, 26, 33, 39, 40, 42, 50, 56, 64, 66 and 67) are reproduced by kind permission of OCR.

The author is responsible for the answers/commentaries on the questions: they have neither been provided nor approved by AQA, Edexcel or OCR and they may not necessarily constitute the only possible solutions.

Blackwell Publishers for extract from *Europe Transformed, 1878–1919* by Norman Stone (1999). ITPS Ltd for extract from Stephen J. Lee *The European Dictatorships 1918–1945* (Routledge, 1987); for extract from Erich Eyck *Bismarck after 50 years* (Routledge, 1961); and for extract from Stephen J. Lee *Imperial Germany 1871–1918* (Routledge, 1999). Hodder & Stoughton for permission to use the extract from *Rivalry and Accord: International relations 1870–1914* by John Lowe (1988) and the extract from *War and Revolution 1914–1917* by Michael Lynch (1992). Extract from Peter Waldron, *The End of Imperial Russia, 1855–1917*, 1997, Macmillan Press reproduced with permission of Palgrave. The extract from *A History of Europe* Norman Davies published by Pimlico. Used by permission of The Random House Group Limited.

Every effort has been made to contact the holders of copyright material, but if any have been inadvertently overlooked, the Publishers will be pleased to make the necessary arrangements at the first opportunity.

Illustrations
Cartoon artwork – Roger Penwill

Photographs
The publishers would like to thank the following for permission to reproduce photographs:
Hulton Archive, page 23; Mary Evans Picture Library, 28 and 60; David King Collection, 37.

How this book will help you
by Derrick Murphy

Exam practice – how to answer questions better

This book will help you to improve your performance in your AS Modern European History exam.

When you answer exam questions, it is vital that what you write is not only factually correct but that it also answers the question on the exam paper. In other words, to get full marks in AS History you need to do two things:

- **show what you know about the subject**
- **show what you can do with your knowledge in answer to the question.**

Candidates underachieve in AS exams, not because they do not know enough facts, but because they do not deal with different types of questions in the most effective way. **This book will help you improve your exam technique.**

Chapter 1 – step-by-step guidance

The first chapter is on Nazi Germany. It aims to give you the practical guidance that will enable you to provide top-quality answers to the questions in subsequent chapters – and in your exam.

❶ How to tackle the question

The author gives you help with:
- understanding the way in which the examiner has written the question (see the later section on p.5 about 'types of exam question')
- deciding how much to write based on the marks available
- planning your answers to questions worth lots of marks

❷ Student's answer to the exam question

The author provides a typical answer to each question. This is not a perfect answer but one which reflects the type of mistakes and misunderstandings that lots of students make when answering such exam questions.

❸ How to score full marks

The author goes through the student's answer highlighting where the student has lost marks and explaining what you would need to do to score full marks for a similar question.

❹ Don't forget

The author provides a checklist of things you MUST do when answering particular types of questions.

Exam practice — questions for you to try

Chapters 2–10

Each chapter is based on a specific area of content. In each chapter there is a question from **AQA, Edexcel and OCR** on the topic, so you are bound to find a question that is relevant to you.

Before you try answering the question, **read through the 'How to score full marks' section. This tells you how to tackle each part of the question and gives guidance on what should go into your answer.**

When you have written your answer, turn to the back of the book **and read through the answer given, which is one that would have scored high marks.** Compare your answer with this. It will not be the same as your answer, but you need to decide whether your answer is as good in all respects. If not, **decide which aspects of exam technique you need to improve on. Look back at Chapter 1, if necessary.**

How questions are marked

Regardless of which exam board sets your paper, your answers will be marked by a **level-of-response mark scheme**. This means that your answer will be awarded a particular level within the mark scheme. Each level is sub-divided into specific marks. Your mark within a particular level will depend on factors such as:

- the depth of your factual knowledge
- your ability to assess and analyse
- the quality of your written English.

Questions worth 3 marks

These usually have two levels of response. Level 1 is for simplistic answers, which are awarded 1 mark. Level 2 answers have relevant factual knowledge and understanding, and contain a developed response. These will be awarded 2 or 3 marks.

Questions worth 5–7 marks (10–15 marks in OCR)

The questions are usually divided into three levels of response.

Questions worth 20–25 marks (60 marks at OCR)

These are usually divided into five levels of response. To achieve the highest levels, you are expected to offer analysis and assessment supported by sound factual knowledge. Depending on the specific question you may also have to:

- use source material which is provided on the examination paper
- refer to different historical interpretations associated with the subject content.

Always remember to answer the question on the paper precisely and concisely. Straightforward narrative or description usually achieves only low to moderate marks. High marks invariably involve some degree of analysis and assessment.

The types of exam question vary from exam board to exam board. However, the main types of questions are listed below, with advice on how to score high marks.

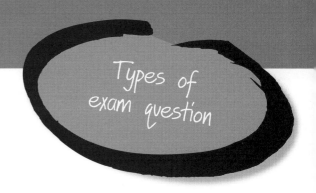

Types of exam question

Type of question	How to get high marks	Common mistakes
Describe: usually with the command instruction 'what'	Make sure your knowledge is specific and relevant.	Unspecific knowledge 'Story telling'
Explanation: 'explain why' questions.	Organise your answer and place reasons in order of importance. Try to identify links between reasons.	Listing points without explanation
Explaining the importance of a historical term.	Explain the meaning of the term and use your own knowledge to place it in historical context, i.e. explain why it is important.	Description without explanation
Interpretation and analysis: 'how far' or 'do you agree or disagree' questions.	Assessment and analysis, supported by relevant factual knowledge.	Narrative and description with some assessment at the end.
Assessing the utility or reliability of a source	Explain the strengths and limitations of the source as evidence. Use outside knowledge to test reliability.	Description of source
Comparing sources	Cross-reference information between sources. Quote from sources to support your case. Remember to compare and contrast information in the sources.	Describing each source in turn. Failure to compare and contrast.
Answering a question using sources and own knowledge to offer an assessment or evaluation.	Integrate information from own knowledge and the sources to produce a balanced assessment.	Using the sources and own knowledge separately. Not using all the sources required by the question. Describing the sources, not evaluating them.

The grid below will help you to identify the questions in each chapter that relate to the modules you are taking for your exam.

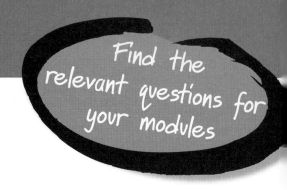
Find the relevant questions for your modules

Chapter	AQA	Edexcel	OCR
1 Nazi Germany	Unit 1 Alternative J: 'The Origins and Consolidation of Totalitarian Regimes 1918–1939'	Unit 3: 'Life in Nazi Germany'	Unit 1: 'National Socialist Germany'
2 The Unification of Germany 1850–1871	Unit 1 Alternative G: 'Imperial and Weimar Germany 1866–1925'	Unit 3: 'Bismarck and the Unification of Germany 1848–1871'	Unit 3: 'Europe 1825–1890'
3 Germany 1870–1914	Unit 1 Alternative E: 'Germany and Russia before the First World War 1870–1914' Unit 1 Alternative G: 'Imperial and Weimar Germany 1866–1925'		Unit 3: 'Europe 1825–1890'
4 Russia 1855–1917	Unit 1 Alternative F: 'Tsarist and Revolutionary Russia 1855–1917'	Unit 1: 'Russia in Revolution 1905–1917'	Unit 3: 'Europe 1890–1945 (Russia 1894–1917)'
5 International Relations 1890–1939	Unit 1 Alternative H: 'The Emergence of the Super Powers and the New World Order 1900–1962'		Unit 3: 'Europe 1890–1945: The causes and Impact of the First World War: 1890–1920' 'Europe and the World 1919–1989: International Relations 1919–1939'
6 Russia/USSR 1917–1929	Unit 3 Alternative F: (a) 'Revolutionary Russia 1917–1929' (b) 'Stalin's Rise to Power 1922–1929' Unit 3 Alternative J: 'The Accession to Power of Bolsheviks and Lenin's Regime'	Unit 2: 'Triumph of Bolshevism? Russia 1918–1929'	
7 USSR 1928–1941	Unit 1 Alternative J: 'The Origins and Consolidation of Totalitarian Regimes'	Unit 3: 'Life in the Soviet Union 1928–1941'	Unit 3: 'Europe and the World 1919–1989: The USSR 1924–1953'
8 Italy 1918–1939	Unit 1 Alternative J: 'The Origins and Consolidation of Totalitarian Regimes'	Unit 2: 'Italy: The Rise of Fascism in Italy 1918–1925'	Unit 3: 'Italy 1919–1939'
9 Germany 1918–1933	Unit 1 Alternative G: 'Imperial and Weimar Germany'	Unit 1: 'The Seeds of Evil: The Rise of National Socialism in Germany to 1933'	Unit 3: 'Germany 1919–1945'
10 The Cold War	Unit 1 Alternative L: 'US Foreign Policy 1890–1991'		Unit 3: 'Europe and the World 1919–1989: 3 The Cold War in Europe 1945–1989 4 The Cold War in Asia and the Americas 1949–1975'

1 Nazi Germany

This chapter contains students' answers to three exam questions – one each from AQA, Edexcel and OCR. There is advice on how to tackle each question in order to maximise your chances of scoring full marks.

The students' answers are 'C' grade answers – in other words, fairly typical ones. The 'How to score full marks' comments after the students' answers point out where marks are gained and lost. This should help you to gain a clear picture of what examiners are looking for in answers to each type of question.

The 'Don't forget …' boxes summarise what you need to do in order to answer each type of question successfully, so that you gain high marks.

Chapters 2–10 contain questions for you to try answering so that you can apply what you have learnt in this chapter.

AQA Exam Question and Student's Answer

This question is taken from **AQA Alternative J Unit 1 on 'The Origins and Consolidation of Totalitarian Regimes 1918–1939'**.

Read the following source and then answer the questions that follow.

> **Adapted from *The European Dictatorships 1918–1945* by Stephen J. Lee (published in 1987)**
>
> Almost all the great personalities of the inter-war period were critics of democracy. The masses were tempted by their charisma, sweeping promises and simple solutions.

(a) What was meant by 'critics of democracy' in relation to the rise of inter-war totalitarian regimes? [3 marks]

(b) Explain why the one-party state was established in Germany in the inter-war period. [7 marks]

(c) 'The role of Hitler was the most important factor in the development of the one-party state in Germany in the inter-war period.'

Explain why you agree or disagree with this statement. [15 marks]

The question above is one of two which you will be expected to answer in a 1 hour 30 minute examination. Therefore, you should spend around 45 minutes on this question.

How to tackle this question

- As part **(a)** is worth only 3 out of a total of 25 marks, spend approximately 5 minutes on this question. To **explain** this term, **in its historical context**, you will be expected to write a paragraph of two or three sentences at most.

- Part **(b)** is worth 7 marks, so you should spend around 15 minutes on your answer. You are expected **to provide reasons** for the establishment of a one-party state in Germany.

  Divide your answer up into separate paragraphs. Write a paragraph for each reason. Remember to place the reasons in order of importance. Always identify the main reason and support your view with factual knowledge. If possible, try to identify links between reasons.

- Part **(c)** carries the most marks [15], so you should spend about 25 minutes on this answer. To ensure that you organise your answer effectively, **make a BRIEF PLAN**. This plan needs to begin with a list of reasons that would support the view that Hitler was '**the most important factor**' in the creation of a one-party state. These may include:
  - his policies
  - his skills as a public speaker
  - his skill and ruthlessness at removing opponents.

  These should be followed by a list of **any other factors** you believe helped to create a one-party state. These could include the:

  - role of other Nazi leaders such as Goring, Himmler and Gobbels
  - fear of communism
  - weakness of democracy
  - support of the army
  - use of terror through the SS.

  You need to divide your answer into a section that **explains** the importance of Hitler and a separate section that **identifies and explains** the other factors.

  You should structure your answer like this:

  > - A brief introduction – one sentence is fine – explaining what you are going to discuss.
  >
  > - An explanation of the importance of the role of Hitler. This may be divided into separate paragraphs, which deal with different parts of Hitler's role.
  >
  > - An explanation of other reasons for the establishment of a one-party state in Germany.
  >
  > - A concluding paragraph that evaluates the importance of Hitler's role, as compared with the importance of the other factors. From the evidence you have produced you may say that, on the whole, you either agree or disagree with the statement made in the question – you must do one or the other or you will lose marks.

TOM'S ANSWERS

(a) What was meant by 'critics of democracy' in relation to the rise of inter-war totalitarian regimes?

Critics of democracy, as mentioned in the extract, refers to the opponents of democracy in Germany during the inter-war period. This took place during the Weimar period of 1918 to 1933 and came from both the extreme left and extreme right of German politics. The main critics were the Nazis on the right and the Communists on the left.

2/3

(b) Explain why the one-party state was established in Germany in the inter-war period.

A one-party state was created in Germany in the inter-war period for a number of reasons.

An economic depression which took place in Germany from 1929. The massive rise in unemployment undermined the democratic government of Weimar Germany. It led to an increase in popularity of extremist parties such as the Nazis and the Communists.

The Nazis used the economic depression to put forward the view that democracy had weakened Germany and the democratic parties such as the SPD were enemies of the German people. Their support for the destruction of the Treaty of Versailles and the rearmament of Germany were popular. So was their anti-Jewish and anti-Communist policies.

However, there were other reasons such as the weakness of coalition government in Weimar Germany. After 1930 no government received majority support in the Reichstag (parliament). This meant that the aged President Hindenburg chose the Chancellor. Hindenburg disliked democracy. Eventually, in January 1933, he chose Hitler as the new Chancellor. This paved the way for one-party rule.

4/7

(c) 'The role of Hitler was the most important factor in the development of the one-party state in Germany in the inter-war period.'
Explain why you agree or disagree with this statement.

Hitler was important in the creation of a one-party state in Germany. In 1928 the Nazis had only a small number of seats in the Reichstag. However, in 1929, the depression began. This led to mass unemployment. The unemployed lost faith in democracy and looked for a radical alternative. Hitler was important because he was a very effective speaker. He toured the country in the elections of 1930 and 1932. He was also clever at opposing communism, the Jews and the Versailles Treaty.

In 1932 the Nazis became the largest political party in Germany. Hitler did well in the presidential elections of that year. Hitler was clever at persuading conservative politicians and the aged President Hindenburg to appoint him as Chancellor in January 1933.

Once he became chancellor Hitler used the Reichstag Fire to ban the Communists. After the March 1933 elections he acquired dictatorial powers with the Enabling Act. Hitler used the act to turn Germany into a Nazi state. Political opponents were placed in concentration camps.

Hitler was also important because he removed opposition from within the Nazi Party. On 30 June 1934, in the Night of the Long Knives, he removed the leadership of the Stormtroopers (SA). Ernst Rohm and other SA leaders were murdered.

Therefore, Hitler can be seen as the most important reason for the creation of a one-party state in Germany. His political skill and ruthlessness created a Nazi dictatorship.

10/15

How to score full marks

Part (a)

🎯 The student, Tom, has placed the term **in its historical context**. He refers **directly** to the Weimar period and provides **dates to support the answer**. Tom is also able to identify the main critics of democracy.

🎯 To score the third mark, Tom needed **to go into more detail**. He needed to say that the Nazis criticised democratic countries for signing the Treaty of Versailles and humiliating Germany through accepting disarmament and reparations. The Communists criticised democratic countries because they felt they exploited their working classes.

Part (b)

🎯 Tom has produced **a structured explanation** of the reasons for the creation of a one-party state. The answer is divided into **separate paragraphs**. **Several reasons** are identified.

🎯 The student fails to gain full marks because **he has not placed these reasons in order of importance**.

🎯 **Tom's answer is also incomplete** because it ends in January 1933 when Germany was still a multi-party state. Hitler led a coalition of Nazis, Conservatives and Nationalists. Only with the Reichstag Fire and the Enabling Act that followed was Hitler able to achieve a one-party state.

Part (c)

🎯 Tom's answer is divided into **separate paragraphs**, which deal with **different aspects** of Hitler's rise to power and the creation of a Nazi dictatorship. **There is a high standard of written English**.

🎯 The answer loses marks mainly because it is not **balanced**. It does not **evaluate** whether Hitler was 'the most important factor', as asked by the question. It relies almost entirely on an explanation of Hitler's role. **It doesn't consider other reasons** for the creation of a one-party state, such as fear of communism or the weakness of democracy. In a question like this, at least 40% of the answer should have been given over to coverage of other factors.

The answer to this question should **not** have been written in a narrative style where the student goes through events in chronological order. A better, more structured answer would first have explained Hitler's role and then gone on to examine other factors.

The answer also fails to gain full marks because **it is rather limited in factual evidence to support the points made**. More detail should have been given, for example, about Hitler's role as an orator during the period 1930–1932.

Overall, Tom achieved a mark of 16 out of 25 for the whole of this question, which would be a 'C' grade.

Don't forget ...

Always write a **brief plan** – a short list of points to be covered – for any question that is worth a lot of marks.

If a question asks you whether you think **one factor** is 'the most important', you must discuss this factor but also ensure you give sufficient coverage to other factors too (at least 40% of your essay).

If a question asks you whether you **'agree or disagree'** with a statement, then you must do one or the other – and be clear about your reasons.

If you are giving a number of reasons, **write a separate paragraph about each reason**.

Make sure you do **explain**, rather than merely *describe*, when you are asked to evaluate different factors.

Make sure you include enough detail in your answer to show the examiner that you have **depth to your historical knowledge** – examiners expect more detail at AS than at GCSE.

This question is taken from **Unit 3 of the Edexcel Specification 'Life in Nazi Germany 1933–1939'**.

Study Source 1 below and then answer questions (a)–(c) which follow.

SOURCE 1

Norman Taylor, an American expert on Germany, writing in the magazine *Foreign Affairs*, in 1936.

Under the Nazis there has been much 'invisible unemployment'. The number of unemployed Jews is great but these are not counted as unemployed. Another source of 'invisible unemployment' has been the wholesale discharge from paid work of women whose husbands are employed, and of unmarried men under twenty-five. None of these are included among the unemployed in the official statistics. Part-time workers are counted fully employed. 'Artificially created' work accounts for some of the employment. The reintroduction of conscription has taken hundreds of thousands of men off the labour market. In 1935 came the increase in employment due to rearmament: this of course is dependent on the continuance of rearmament at the same lively rate.

(a) Study Source 1.
How highly does the author of this source rate the achievements of Nazi economic policy in the years 1933–1936? Explain your answer. [5 marks]

(b) What, in the years 1933 to 1939, were the main aims of Nazi economic policy? [7 marks]

(c) Did the lives of the mass of the German people improve or worsen as a result of the Nazis' economic policies? Explain your answer. [18 marks]

How to tackle this question

- You have 1 hour to answer the paper. Spend approximately 10 minutes on part (a) as it is worth 5 marks – one-sixth of the 30 marks available from the three questions. This question asks you 'how highly' the author rates the achievements. **You need to answer this directly**. You could write one paragraph **identifying evidence of support** for Nazi policies and **another paragraph on the author's criticism** of Nazi policy.

- You are asked to explain your answer so **it is important to quote from the source to support the views you make**.

- Spend approximately 15 minutes answering part (b). You are expected to **use your own knowledge to explain** the main aims of Nazi economic policy. **Write a separate paragraph on each aim**.

- As part (c) carries 18 marks, you should spend approximately 35 minutes on this question. It is important to structure your answer effectively. Therefore, **make a BRIEF PLAN or list**:

  — ways in which the lives of the mass of Germans was improved by Nazi economic policies, e.g. fall in unemployment;

  — ways in which the policies may have worsened their lives, e.g. fall in the standard of living of those in work...

- Write a short introduction – one sentence is enough. Then write a separate paragraph on each point you make. Remember, you are asked to make **an analytical judgement about the consequences** of Nazi economic policy. Therefore, you will be expected to write a **BALANCED account with evidence** of where people's lives improved and where they were worse off as a result of these policies.

SARAH'S ANSWERS

(a) Study Source 1.

How highly does the author of this source rate the achievements of Nazi economic policy in the years 1933–1936? Explain your answer.

In Source 1 the American author, Norman Taylor, doesn't rate Nazi achievements highly. He believes their policies have thrown loads of people out of work and have created invisible unemployment.

2/5

(b) What, in the years 1933 to 1939, were the main aims of Nazi economic policy?

The main aim of Nazi economic policy was to reduce unemployment. When the Nazis took power, in 1933, unemployment was very high. The level of unemployment had helped the Nazis get into power. To achieve less unemployment Hitler created the National Labour Service which recruited thousands of unemployed into work gangs that helped build the autobahns across Germany. He also removed Jews from the workforce.

The Nazis also wanted to rearm Germany. Hitler wanted to destroy the Treaty of Versailles. As part of this plan he hoped to rearm Germany. This would require considerable spending on armaments.

5/7

(c) Did the lives of the mass of the German people improve or worsen as a result of the Nazis' economic policies? Explain your answer.

The Nazis changed the lives of Germans in a number of ways. Firstly, they reduced unemployment and gave many Germans hope after years of despair. Armaments factories and motorway (autobahn) construction provided thousands of jobs. By 1936 Germany had almost full employment. The German Labour service provided jobs, so did the re-introduction of conscription.

The Nazis also changed the lives of women. A woman's place was in the home bringing up the new generation of Germans. They were forced to leave work. This is mentioned in Source 1. Other Germans also suffered, in particular Jews who were forced to leave employment. Jewish shops were boycotted in 1933. Later, the Nuremberg Laws took away German citizenship. The Jews became a persecuted minority.

Trade unionists also suffered. Free trade unions were abolished in 1933. All workers were forced to join the German Labour Front. Under the Nazis the standard of living fell for many workers. Goring had said that the Germans had to choose between guns and butter. Rearmament meant less consumer goods. So for most Germans life was made worse by the Nazis.

12/18

How to score full marks

Part (a)

🎯 This answer addresses only a limited amount of the material that is contained in the source. Although Sarah identifies the issue of invisible unemployment, she does **not explain in enough detail what this is**. She should have made direct reference to the position of Jews, women and young military conscripts.

🎯 To gain full marks, Sarah also needed to highlight the fact that the author did appreciate that the Nazis achieved a major drop in unemployment associated with rearmament, although he wondered how long this would last.

🎯 Sarah should have taken a few short quotes from the source to support her arguments.

Part (b)

🎯 This answer **identifies two aims** of economic policy. It is divided into paragraphs **which helps to order the ideas**. It **highlights** the issue of unemployment that appears in Source 1 and mentions the need to rearm.

🎯 To gain the further two marks, Sarah needed to mention the additional aim of creating a war economy through economic self-sufficiency (autarky) which was inaugurated in the Four Year Plan of 1936.

Part (c)

🎯 Sarah has written in separate paragraphs which **helps the examiner to follow the argument** which is being put forward. The answer is **entirely focused on the demands of the question** and does not contain irrelevant information. (If you do put irrelevant information into your answer you will not be penalised but you will not be awarded any marks for it so it is a waste of valuable time to stray from the demands of the question.)

🎯 However, the explanation is too **one-sided to score high marks**. The first paragraph does deal with improvements in the lives of Germans but thereafter the answer only focuses on the way in which lives were changed for the worse.

🎯 To gain higher marks, **the answer needs to be a more balanced account**. This is how a more balanced account could have been structured:

> *Paragraph 1:* explain how the rapid reduction of unemployment removed economic misery and hopelessness and brought political and economic stability.
>
> *Paragraph 2:* explain that the reduction of unemployment led to an increase in the general standard of living of the mass of Germans.
>
> *Paragraph 3:* explain how rearmament and the creation of the war economy led to a fall in the availability of consumer goods.
>
> *Paragraph 4:* explain how Germans were worse off because of the loss of free trade unions and the reintroduction of compulsory military service for all adult males from 1935.
>
> *Conclusion:* a clear summary of whether, in your opinion, the German people were on balance better or worse off. Support this with brief references back to the reasons given in your earlier paragraphs.

The answer also contains **too little detailed factual knowledge**. It should have included the following:

- The degree of unemployment fell under the Nazis. In January 1933, when Hitler was appointed Chancellor, the unemployment level was 6 million – approximately 1 in 4 of the workforce. This fell dramatically during the Nazi period in power. By 1936 it had fallen to 1.5 million and by 1938 it was under 500,000.

- Those young men who were out of work in January 1933 were forced to join the National Labour Service (RAD). They wore uniforms and were the main workforce that built the autobahn (motorway) network. In addition, compulsory military conscription was reintroduced in March 1935. Therefore, all young adult males had to serve in the armed forces.

- On 2 May 1933, the Nazis abolished the free trade union movement. In its place was the German Labour Force (DAF). This was directly under the control of the Nazi Party. In July 1933 DAF had a membership of 5.3 million. This rose to 21 million by 1935.

- As part of the Nazi attempt to build a German National Community, known as Volksgemeinschaft, women were strongly encouraged to follow the KKK principle of Kinder (children), Kirche (church) and Kuche (cooking). Women were encouraged to give up employment. Their main task was to act as mothers to the next generation of Germans. They were expected to have as many children as possible. A medal – the Honour or Mother's Cross – was awarded by Hitler for any German woman who had several children. A gold cross was awarded to women who had more than eight children. In addition, contraception was restricted and abortion outlawed.

- The development of a police state affected the lives of the majority of Germans. The press was controlled, and the cinema and radio were run by Gobbels' Ministry of Propaganda. The Gestapo (secret police) arrested any critics of the regime. Thousands were sent to concentration camps such as Dachau near Munich.

- The education of children was changed dramatically. Subjects such as History and Biology extolled the greatest of Germans and the superiority of the German race.

Overall, Sarah received 19 out of 30 marks – which is a 'C' grade response.

Don't forget ...

In a question that asks about a given source, you should **make direct reference to it in your answer** – lifting short quotes if this helps your explanation.

If you are asked to explain aims or objectives, **use a different paragraph for each one**. Make sure you do write about ALL the relevant aims or objectives. You will lose marks if you miss one out as the examiner's mark scheme will specify that **a full mark answer should cover all of them**.

If you are asked for your opinion on a matter, **you must deal with both sides of the argument**. You must give reasons for and against and then **sum up your overall opinion in your conclusion**.

This question is taken from **Unit 1 on 'National Socialist Germany 1933–1945'**.

Hitler's claims about German interests

SOURCE A

Hitler appeals to the nation. Adapted from Hitler's 'Appeal to the German People', January 1933.

The National Government will therefore regard it as its first and supreme task to restore to the German people a unity of mind and will. It will take under its firm protection Christianity as the basis of German morality, and the family as the nucleus of the German nation and the German state. It will bring back to our people the consciousness of its racial and political unity. It wishes to base the education of German youth on respect for our great German past. Germany must not and will not sink into communist anarchy. In place of our turbulent instincts, it will make national discipline govern our life.

The National Government will carry out the great task of reorganising and developing our national economy with two big Four Year Plans: it will save the German farmer so that the nation's food supply, and thus the life of the nation, shall be secured; it will save the German worker by a massive attack on unemployment.

SOURCE B

Hitler speaks of the future, from a speech to Reich Governors, July 1933.

The political parties have now been abolished. The achievement of outward power must be followed by the inward education of man. Revolution is not a permanent state; it must not develop into a lasting state. The full spate of revolution must now be guided into the secure bed of national evolution. We must not keep looking round to see what next to revolutionise. The main thing now is not the programme or ideas but the daily bread of five million German people.

SOURCE C

Hitler reassures France after remilitarising the Rhineland – from a speech to the Reichstag, March 1936.

You know how hard was the road that I have had to travel since 30 January 1933 in order to free the German people from the dishonourable position in which it found itself.

At no moment of my struggle on behalf of the German people have I forgotten the duty incumbent on me to uphold European cultures and European civilisation.

The German people have no interest in seeing the French people suffer. Why should it not be possible to lift the problem of conflicting interests between the European states above the sphere of passion and unreason and consider it in the calm of a higher vision?

SOURCE D

Hitler sets his targets – adapted from Hitler's Memorandum issued August 1936.

The world has been moving with ever-increasing speed towards a new conflict, the solution of which is the crushing of Bolshevism.

I thus set the following essential tasks:

    1 The German armed forces must be operational within four years.

    2 The German economy must be fit for war within four years.

(a) Study Source B.
From this source and your own knowledge, explain why, in the summer of 1933, Hitler was keen to stress that 'Revolution is not a permanent state; it must not develop into a lasting state.' (**lines 2–3**)   **[10 marks]**

(b) Study Source A.
How completely does this source reveal Hitler's intentions as leader of Germany in January 1933?   **[25 marks]**

(c) Study Sources C and D.
Compare Hitler's intentions and aims in 1936 as shown in these sources and explain the differences.   **[25 marks]**

(d) Study all the sources.
Using all these sources and your own knowledge, explain Hitler's aims and priorities as leader of Germany in the period 1933 to 1939.   **[60 marks]**

Total marks: 120

How to tackle this question

- You have 1 hour 15 minutes to answer the whole question. Spend approximately 7 minutes on part **(a)**. You are asked **to explain the meaning** of the phrase, **in the historical context** of the period. You will need to use **appropriate quotes from the source and your own knowledge** to achieve full marks. **You must explain, not describe!**

- Spend approximately 12 minutes on part **(b)**. You are asked to explain '**how completely**' this source reveals Hitler's intentions. Therefore, you must identify **both its strengths and weaknesses** as a source in this respect. You must also include **a personal judgement of the degree to which it reveals Hitler's intentions** if you want to achieve full marks.

- Spend approximately 12 minutes on part **(c)**. You are asked **to compare** two sources. Therefore, **you will need to quote from both sources to support your answer**. To achieve full marks, **you must also explain why these two sources are different**.

- Spend around 40 minutes on part **(d)** as this is worth 60 marks – half the total marks available for the whole question. It is important that you make **a BRIEF PLAN** where **you decide how you are going to integrate information from the sources with your knowledge**. This is how such a plan might look:

  — Sources A and B deal with the domestic aims and priorities of Hitler at the beginning of his rule. These two aims are important in 1933 because Hitler had to end political conflict and, in particular, end the threat of communism. Hitler also had to ensure that the economy recovered. He had got into power because of mass unemployment. President Hindenburg could have dismissed him if he failed to deal with this issue.

  — Sources C and D deal with foreign policy aims. Dated 1936, these sources illustrate that after consolidating his hold on political power in Germany, Hitler now planned to destroy the Versailles settlement and prepare for a war against the USSR in East Europe.

- In addition, you will need to supplement **material from the four sources with your own knowledge**. For instance, in domestic affairs Hitler wanted to establish a dictatorship which meant the end to democratic government. This was mainly achieved in the period of 'Forced Coordination' (Gleichshaltung) between January 1933 and August 1934. He also wanted to build a German National Community (Volksgemeinschaft). This involved trying to create a class German society with emphasis on increasing the population and removing minority groups that Hitler disliked (such as Jews, homosexuals and the handicapped). In foreign policy, you will need to explain Hitler's aims of destroying the Versailles settlement, uniting all Germans in one state and, most importantly, 'living space' (lebensraum) in the East. This would involve a war of annihilation against the USSR. In achieving this end you need to refer to the remilitarisation of the Rhineland in 1936, the Anschluss with Austria in March 1938 and the Sudetenland crisis of September 1938.

TANYA'S ANSWERS

(a) Study Source B.

From this source and your own knowledge, explain why, in the summer of 1933, Hitler was keen to stress that 'Revolution is not a permanent state; it must not develop into a lasting state.' **(lines 2–3)**

In the summer of 1933 Hitler made the statement that 'revolution was not a permanent state' because he wished to prevent any new revolutionary changes. He had created a one-party state and made himself the undisputed leader of Germany. However, he feared the Stormtroopers wanted to start a second revolution which would involve social as well as political changes.

(b) Study Source A.

How completely does this source reveal Hitler's intentions as leader of Germany in January 1933?

Source A offers a lot of information about Hitler's intentions as leader of Germany in January 1933. Hitler was against communism and was a strong German nationalist. He disliked the way Germany had been treated at the Treaty of Versailles. In that treaty Germany lost a lot of land and had its army reduced to 100,000.

Hitler also believed that the Weimar Republic provided Germany with very weak government. After 1930 no government had majority support in the German parliament. Also, because of mass unemployment Germany was divided into hostile groups.

As the source states, Hitler wanted to restore national unity and to protect Christianity and the family. He also wanted to restore the education of German youth and to reorganise the economy through Four Year plans. Finally, he wanted to protect German farmers and German workers.

All these reasons mentioned in the source show what Hitler wanted to achieve when he got into power in January 1933.

(c) Study Sources C and D.

Compare Hitler's intentions and aims in 1936 as shown in these sources and explain the differences.

In Source C, a speech given in 1936, Hitler gives the distinct impression that he wants to make peace with France and to protect Europe from future wars. He suggests that the remilitarisation of the Rhineland is a just act. In the Treaty of Versailles, Germany was forced to accept a massive reduction in its armed forces. It was also forced to suffer an army of occupation and was forbidden to place German troops in the Rhineland. Hitler uses this speech to try to reassure the French — and other countries — that he does not plan to invade France and all that Germany wants is to place troops within a part of Germany.

Source D is very different from Source C. Hitler is seen preparing for war. He plans to have the army and economy ready within four years, that is by 1940. This source shows that Hitler is really very aggressive in foreign policy. He does not want peace. He wants war. He says he dislikes Bolshevism and wants to go to war to destroy it. Hitler really wants to unite all Germans into one state and wants to take over eastern Europe as living space (Lebensraum) for the German people. This shows that Hitler does not want European peace at all.

(d) Study all the sources.

Using all these sources and your own knowledge, explain Hitler's aims and priorities as leader of Germany in the period 1933 to 1939.

Hitler had many aims and priorities. He wanted to end mass unemployment and make Germany a strong and prosperous country again after the Depression. He also hated the treaty of Versailles. He wanted Germany to rearm and to reunite all Germans into one large German Empire. He also wanted living space in eastern Europe. This would involve going to war to conquer lands in the East.

The sources show Hitler's aims and intention. Source A shows that Hitler wanted to bring the German people together. He wanted a strong nation. He says 'the National Government regards it as its first and supreme task to restore to the German people a unity of mind and will'. In Source B he also says he wants to prevent further revolution in Germany. He says 'the full spate of revolution must now be guided into the secure bed of national evolution. We must not keep looking around to see what next to revolutionise.' This means he wanted to prevent the Stormtroopers under Ernst Rohm starting another revolution. He wanted to prevent Rohm creating a people's militia from the Stormtroopers which would have replaced the German army. Hitler needed the army to achieve living space in the East. In June 1934 he used the SS to murder the leaders of the Stormtroopers. This brought to an end the chance of a second revolution. Hitler was now the one dictator of Germany.

In Source C, after remilitarising the Rhineland Hitler attempts to reassure the French that he does not plan to attack them. This was not really true. Hitler wanted to unite all Germans and to gain Lebensraum or living space in the East. This would involve invading Poland and the USSR. In 1938 he took over Austria, followed by the Sudetenland in September 1938. By 1939 he had occupied the Czech lands. He did not plan to attack the West. It was Britain and France who declared war on Germany in 1939.

As Source D states Hitler planned a war in the east to destroy communism. He makes clear in Source D that he was planning this from 1936.

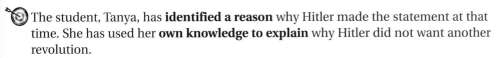

How to score full marks

Part (a)

🎯 The student, Tanya, has **identified a reason** why Hitler made the statement at that time. She has used her **own knowledge to explain** why Hitler did not want another revolution.

🎯 **The explanation given is valid but incomplete**. To score the extra TWO marks, the answer would also need to have dealt with the major issue of unemployment, which is mentioned towards the end of the source.

Part (b)

🎯 Tanya places the source in **historical context** and links this with information from the source.

🎯 **The main reason this answer only scores 15 marks is that the student uses the source uncritically**. The question asks 'how completely' the source reveals Hitler's intentions. This is a major clue that **you need to weigh up the reliability** of the source in your answer.

🎯 The source is a speech of Hitler's – **your answer needs to address what his aims were in making it and why he might not have spoken about all his intentions**. To score high marks, your answer needs to explain that Hitler was making a public appeal to the German people. He wanted to unify them and to stop internal squabbling. He did not want to frighten them by talk of war. This source does NOT, therefore, paint a complete picture of Hitler's intentions. At this date, January 1933, Hitler does not mention any of his intentions in foreign affairs such as the destruction of the Treaty of Versailles, and the unification of all Germans in one state or Lebensraum.

Part (c)

🎯 This answer **is clearly focused on the question**. It deals not only with the content of both sources but also provides relevant factual knowledge that helps to explain Hitler's motives.

🎯 What Tanya does not do is **evaluate each source as a type of historical evidence**. This is what explains their different tone and message, although both sources date from the same year.

🎯 Tanya should have mentioned the possible motive behind Source C. Having reoccupied the Rhineland, Hitler didn't want to antagonise the French. So, in **public**, he tried to give the impression of a man of peace. Tanya should also have mentioned that Source D was a **private** memorandum and, as such, was more likely to reveal Hitler's true intentions: to embark on a war of conquest to achieve his aims.

Part (d)

🎯 Tanya identifies **different aspects of Hitler's aims** in all four sources. She sometimes provides relevant **factual knowledge** to support the points she makes. Tanya is able to point out, for example in support of Source B's views, that Hitler is referring to the threat of a second revolution from the Stormtroopers. There is a lack of supporting factual knowledge for Sources C and D.

🎯 Although Tanya identifies Hitler's aims, she does not point out that **Hitler's aims changed in the period 1933–1939**. In 1933 his main priority was to bring about German unity and to repair the economy. By 1936 his aims had changed. He was now interested in foreign policy matters rather than consolidating his control within Germany.

To score high marks, **you need to deal with the sources in groups rather than individually**. Two sources are from 1933 and two are from 1936. If you approach your answer in this way, then it is easy to show how Hitler's aims and intentions changed over time. In 1933 he wanted to return prosperity and unity to Germany and to prevent any further revolutionary outbreaks after he took power. By 1936 his main aims and intentions had changed to foreign policy and the possibility of future war by 1940.

You also need to **refer to the value of each source as evidence of Hitler's intentions and to explain whether it represents an accurate indication of his aims**.

Finally, **you need to include more of your own factual knowledge** in your answer than the student did so that you give **a full historical context to each source**.

Overall, Tanya achieved a mark of 76 out of 120 and was awarded a 'C' grade.

Don't forget ...

In source-based questions, always **quote from the sources** to support your explanations.

Look for clues in questions on sources. For example, if a question asks you 'how completely' you think a source reveals the writer's intentions, then this is a clue that **you need to evaluate the reliability of the source** in your answer.

Always **look carefully at the dates of sources and who has written them**. You need to take these into account if you are asked to make comparisons between them or to explain differences.

Always **think hard about the audience that any particular source is addressed at**. This will help you to decide what its purpose was and how reliable it is as evidence.

Where a question asks you to use the sources **AND your own knowledge**, make sure you do this throughout your answer, integrating the two. Your ability to place the source in **historical context** will be assessed by the examiner.

Remember that written sources often contain **factual evidence** and **opinions**. You need to judge the balance between the two when evaluating the reliability of these sources.

Questions to try

AQA Unit 1 Alternative G: 'Imperial and Weimar Germany 1866–1925'

This question should be answered in 45 minutes.

Study the following source material and then answer the questions that follow.

SOURCE A

A statue of Bismarck

SOURCE B

Adapted from *Bismarck after 50 years* by Erich Eyck, published in 1961

When Bismarck died on 30 July 1890, the German Empire stood splendid in all its strength and power. His spell over the German people was almost boundless and no name filled a gathering of German students more quickly with enthusiasm. His statesmanlike qualities included his courage and patience, the richness and superiority of his intellect, his marvellous understanding of all the persons with whom he had to deal, and his never failing skill in finding a way out of the most difficult and complicated situations.

SOURCE C

Adapted from *A History of Europe* by Norman Davies, 1996

Bismarck's reputation was a mixed one. No one can deny his mastery of the political art; but many question his morality and his intentions. For liberal critics, he was and remains a great and evil man. They see him as an aggressor who used war as a conscious instrument of policy; as a cheat, who introduced democratic forms in order to preserve the undemocratic Prussian establishment; as a bully, who bludgeoned his opponents with the blunt instruments of state power.

(a) Study Source A.
    Using your own knowledge, explain briefly the significance of the way in which Bismarck is represented in the context of the creation of Germany from 1866. [3 marks]

(b) Study Sources B and C.
    With reference to your own knowledge of Bismarck, explain how the view put forward in Source C challenges that put forward in Source B. [7 marks]

(c) Study Sources A, B and C and use your own knowledge.
    Explain the importance, in relation to other factors, of Bismarck's contribution to the unification of Germany from 1866 to 1871. [15 marks]

Total marks: 25

How to score full marks

Before answering this question, look back at the '*Don't forget ...*' section on page 22 which gives advice on how to answer source/document questions successfully.

Part (a)

Don't spend more than **5 minutes** on this. Remember that you have to place this photograph in historical context. Do not merely describe it. Don't forget Bismarck was known as the 'Iron Chancellor' and that he united Germany by armed might not by negotiation. This places Bismarck in marked contrast to the Liberal nationalists in the Frankfurt parliament of 1848–49.

Part (b)

This requires you **to evaluate** the two sources as differing historical interpretations. Your answer must include **an explanation** of why these two historians differ in their view. To support your answer you must **use your own knowledge**.

Part (c)

The key words here are '**in relation to other factors**'. This tells you that **you need to spend about half your answer discussing these other factors**. You also need **to evaluate the relative importance** of Bismarck, as opposed to these other factors (i.e. you need to make a judgement).

Make a **brief plan** on how you are going to organise your answer. This could be along the following lines:

> *Introduction:* brief statement about the importance of Bismarck in the unification of Germany.
>
> *Paragraph 2:* Bismarck's diplomacy before the wars of 1866 and 1870–71, preventing opponents gaining allies.
>
> *Paragraph 3:* Bismarck and the Ems Telegram of 1870.
>
> *Paragraph 4:* role of Napoleon III and the French.
>
> *Paragraph 5:* role of the Prussian army in the wars of 1866 and 1870–71.
>
> *Paragraph 6:* importance of German nationalism.
>
> *Paragraph 7:* importance of rapid industrial change in Germany.
>
> *Conclusion:* your judgement on the relative importance of Bismarck as compared to these other factors.

Integrate **information from the sources** and **your own knowledge** to produce **a BALANCED answer**.

Edexcel Question from Unit 3: 'Bismarck and the Unification of Germany c1848–1871'

Study Source 1 below and then answer the questions (a)–(c) which follow.

SOURCE 1

John Venedy, a liberal politician from Cologne, writing in 1864

Prussia was and is dominated by a political orientation that could not and cannot lead to German unity. If this policy, which has found its archetype in Count Bismarck, conquered Germany tomorrow and unified it by force, then even this conquest of all Germany would not lead to German unity. A conquest of Germany by a Prussia that is not ruled in the German spirit would be merely a bare fact that would last until it was superseded by another fact. The unity of Germany must be founded on something beyond the 'majestic thundering of cannon'; it must be rooted in German respect for law, German popular honour and popular self-government if it is to last. The unity of Germany can be realised only by and with the German people, not by a 'Crown' with the help of a party that scorns German law and German nationality.

(a) Study Source 1.
In what ways does the author of Source 1 criticise Bismarck's methods of achieving German unity? [5 marks]

(b) How did Bismarck, in the years 1864 to 1866, achieve a localised war with Austria? [7 marks]

(c) What factors worked against the inclusion of the Southern states within a united Germany in 1866, but nevertheless worked for their inclusion in 1871? [18 marks]

Total marks: 30

How to score full marks

Part (a)

Spend approximately **5 minutes** on this question. **Use quotations** from the source to support your views but keep them brief and to the point. The question says 'what ways', so the examiner will be looking for you to identify and explain at least 2 or 3 different ways.

Part (b)

Spend approximately **10 minutes** on this question. You are asked to explain how Bismarck made sure the war was only between Prussia and Austria. **Make sure you write a separate paragraph** explaining each of the ways in which he was able to do this. You need to place Bismarck's methods **in order of importance**. Make sure you **limit your answer to the 1864–1866 period**.

Part (c)

Spend approximately **40 minutes** answering this question. Write **a brief plan** to help you organise your answer. It should be along the following lines:

> *Introduction:* a brief statement of what you are going to cover in your answer (e.g. 'There were a number of reasons why Bismarck could not include the Southern states in a united Germany in 1866 but could do so in 1871.')
>
> *Paragraph 2:* first reason why they couldn't be included in 1866 (e.g. the Catholic/Protestant split).
>
> *Paragraph 3:* another reason for non-inclusion in 1866 (e.g. this would have faced opposition from France as inclusion would radically upset the balance of power).
>
> *Paragraph 4:* inclusion in 1871 because of the impact of the war of 1870–71 where North German Confederation and South German States fought France together.
>
> *Paragraph 5:* terms of 1871 Constitution which allowed the Southern states such as Bavaria considerable self-government.

Make sure:

- you write **a balanced answer**. You need to make ample time and space to cover the factors which **excluded** the Southern states in 1866 and the factors which led to their **inclusion** in 1871.

- you **integrate information in Source 1** which refers to the importance of German nationalism in the process of unification.

OCR Question from Unit 2: 'Europe 1825 to 1890'

(a) Explain the economic and political factors which contributed to Prussia's influence in Germany in 1860.

[30 marks]

(b) How important was Bismarck to the achievement of German unity between 1862 and 1871?

[60 marks]

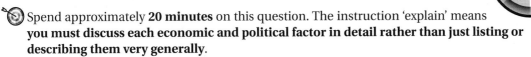

How to score full marks

Part (a)

🎯 Spend approximately **20 minutes** on this question. The instruction 'explain' means **you must discuss each economic and political factor in detail rather than just listing or describing them very generally**.

🎯 Make **a brief plan** on how you are going to organise your answer. This could be along the following lines:

> *Introduction:* brief statement on what you are going to cover, such as 'By 1860 a number of important economic and political factors helped Prussia to increase its influence in Germany.'
>
> *Paragraph 2:* the impact of the Zollverein.
>
> *Paragraph 3:* the impact of the rapid industrialisation of Prussia after 1850.
>
> *Paragraph 4:* the strength of Prussian armed forces.
>
> *Paragraph 5:* the weakness of Austria.
>
> *Conclusion:* summarise the relative importance of each factor.

🎯 Make sure you are able to place the reasons in order of importance.

🎯 Avoid 'telling a story' or describing events. Explain!

Part (b)

🎯 Spend approximately **40 minutes** on this question. The command instruction in the question asks you to evaluate '**how important**' Bismarck was to the achievement of German unity. This means you must explain Bismarck's role and compare it to other factors which helped the achievement of German unity – such as the strength of the Prussian army, the weakness of Austria, the errors of Napoleon III of France and economic factors which were mentioned in part (**a**).

🎯 Write **a brief plan** of how you are going to organise your answer. This could be as follows:

> *Introduction:* a brief statement such as 'In the achievement of German unity Bismarck's role was very important but so were a number of other factors.'
>
> *Paragraph 2:* Bismarck's role in creating a strong conservative government in Prussia from 1862.
>
> *Paragraph 3:* Bismarck's diplomatic role in defeating Denmark and Austria.
>
> *Paragraph 4:* Bismarck's role in isolating France after 1866 and his role in the Ems Telegram.
>
> *Paragraph 5:* explanation of weakness of Austria in 1865–66 and France in 1870.
>
> *Paragraph 6:* explanation of the role of German nationalism.
>
> *Paragraph 7:* explanation of role of economic factors.
>
> *Conclusion:* that summarises the importance of Bismarck as opposed to other factors.

Answers to all of the 'Questions to try' in this chapter can be found on pages 69–71.

Questions to try

AQA Unit 1 Alternative E: 'Germany and Russia before the First World War 1870–1914'

Study the following source material and then answer the questions which follow.

SOURCE A

From a contemporary cartoon, commenting on the Dreikaiserbund of 1873

SOURCE B

Adapted from *Europe in Rivalry and Accord: The Great Powers 1870–1914* by John Lowe, 1988

In 1875, Bismarck's strategy of quietly allaying fears about Germany's dominant position in Europe was suddenly discarded in a crisis with France which he provoked himself. In April, the *Berlin Post* published an article (regarded as government-inspired) under the dramatic heading 'Is war in sight?' It seemed that Bismarck was raising the spectre of war – but for no good reason and with no clear purpose.

SOURCE C

Adapted from *Imperial Germany 1871–1918* by Stephen J. Lee, 1999

By 1890, Bismarck had carefully and systematically put together a system of alliances which, properly used and maintained, would serve the related purposes of keeping Europe at peace and maintaining Germany's position of predominance. Unfortunately, all this was upset by blunders of his successors. In the longer term, it must be admitted, Bismarck's 'system' proved too complex for lesser statesmen to maintain. Criticism of him, therefore, centres not on his failure but rather on his being too clever by half.

(a) Study Source A.
Using your knowledge, explain briefly the importance of the Dreikaiserbund in Bismarck's foreign policy. [3 marks]

(b) Study Sources B and C.
With reference to your own knowledge of German foreign policy, explain how the author of Source C differs in his view of Bismarck's foreign policy from the views made in Source B. [7 marks]

(c) Study Sources A, B and C and use your own knowledge.
How effective was Bismarck's system of alliances in maintaining peace in Europe in the years 1871 to 1890? [15 marks]

Total marks: 25

How to score full marks

Part (a)

To achieve full marks you need to place the Dreikaiserbund **within the context of Bismarck's foreign policy**. By all means mention the signatories and its terms. However, you will have to point out that one of Bismarck's main aims in foreign policy was to isolate France.

Part (b)

This question requires you **to evaluate** the two sources and to explain how they offer different historical interpretations. Source B suggests that Bismarck's decision to embark on the 'war in sight' crisis against France in 1875 was without purpose and reason. Yet Source C suggests Bismarck's policies were carefully and systematically put together to maintain European peace. **You need to use your own knowledge of German foreign policy to explain how these two historians can offer such differing interpretations of events**.

Part (c)

You must organise your answer to produce **a BALANCED assessment**. This will involve, firstly, producing **evidence** to support the view that Bismarck was effective in maintaining peace. Then put the other side of the argument: write down the ways in which Bismarck's policies had the effect of upsetting European peace.

Make sure you use the sources **and** your own knowledge. Try to **integrate** source material and your own knowledge **into the same paragraph**.

From the sources you could mention that Source A shows how Bismarck attempted to isolate France by keeping three of the Great Powers in agreement. This is supported by Source C which states that Bismarck produced a systematic set of alliances and agreements which helped to maintain European peace. Support this with 'own knowledge':

— Europe did not face a Great Power war between 1871—1890. When trouble did break out in the Balkans in 1875—78 and 1885—87, Bismarck helped to solve the crises. His agreements and alliances (Dreikaiserbund 1873 and 1881, Dual Alliance, Triple Alliance, Mediterranean Agreements and Reinsurance Treaty) helped keep the peace and France isolated.

In opposition to this view, Source B suggests Bismarck acted in 1875 for no clear purpose and threatened European peace. Source C states that Bismarck was a very clever politician but his alliance system could not be operated by his successors. Therefore, he left a legacy of potential conflict. You could **use your own knowledge** to mention that the Reinsurance Treaty of 1887 contradicted the Dual Alliance and sooner or later his system of alliances was bound to fall apart. Also, his system of secret alliances increased tension between Europe's Great Powers.

Q2

Read the following source and then answer the questions that follow.

> In 1897, Germany embarked on a 'world policy' (Weltpolitik).
> This policy was not a success for Germany before 1914.

(a) Explain what you understand by the term 'world policy' (Weltpolitik) in relation to German foreign policy after 1897. [3 marks]

(b) Explain why Germany embarked on a 'world policy' (Weltpolitik) after 1897. [7 marks]

(c) Weltpolitik 'was not a success for Germany before 1914'.
Explain why you agree or disagree with this view. [15 marks]

Total marks: 25

How to score full marks

Part (a)

🎯 You will need to explain the meaning of the term **precisely** but also **in the context of German foreign policy**.

Part (b)

🎯 This question requires you to provide reasons for Weltpolitik. To score full marks not only do you have to mention several reasons you also need to place them **in order of importance**.

🎯 You should mention **and expand on** the following points:

- the creation of a world empire seemed a natural progression (Prussia grew into the German Empire and now the German Empire should become a world power)
- the belief in social Darwinism
- the scramble for Africa and territories in Asia
- internal politics (the Kaiser hoped to unite all political groups, except the Socialists, in support of Germany's quest for a large empire).

Part (c)

🎯 The question asks you to explain why you agree or disagree. What the examiners are actually looking for is **a balanced answer**.

- First of all you need to point out where you agree with the statement that Weltpolitik was not a success and then point out where it was successful.
- You will need to mention that Weltpolitik failed to acquire much territory except in the Pacific, China and part of the Cameroons. It also helped to raise international tension. It forced Britain to sign agreements with its former enemies France and Russia, in 1904 and 1907. By 1914 Europe seemed to be divided into two armed camps: on one side was the Triple Alliance; on the other were Russia and France in the Dual Alliance supported by Britain. Weltpolitik also started a naval race with Britain which proved very costly for both nations.
- On the success side you could mention that Germany acquired a world-class navy by 1914, to rival Britain. It did acquire some territory. Finally, for most of the period 1897 to 1914 it united most German political parties behind the government.

AQA Unit 1 Alternative G: 'Imperial and Weimar Germany 1866–1925'

Read the following source and then answer the questions that follow.

Adapted from *Europe Transformed* by Norman Stone, 1999

After the crucial events of 1878–1879, Bismarck maintained complete Conservative dominance in Germany, supported by an 'alliance of Steel and Rye', and was able to virtually ignore opposition from the Liberals, Catholics and Socialists.

(a) Explain what was meant by the 'alliance of Steel and Rye' in relation to Bismarck's domestic policy after 1871. [3 marks]

(b) Explain why the events of 1878–1879 were so significant for the internal political affairs of Germany from 1871 to 1890. [7 marks]

(c) 'The internal strengths of Imperial Germany outweighed its weaknesses at the time of the fall of Bismarck.' Explain why you agree or disagree with this view. [15 marks]

Total marks: 25

How to score full marks

Part (a)

To score full marks you must not only explain the phrase but also place it in **historical context**. This question is marked on a two-level mark scheme. In Level 1 (worth 1 mark) you would be expected to mention that the alliance referred to industrialists and large landowners. To get into Level 2 (2–3 marks) you need to explain that these two groups represented the backbone of support for Bismarck. Steel represented the new industrial elite, while rye represented the old Prussian conservative elite based on the Junker class.

Part (b)

To achieve marks at the highest level (6–7 marks) you need to discuss **several reasons** why these years were a turning point. For example:

- the end of free trade and the introduction of tariffs

- the ending of the Kulturkampf

- the attempted assassination of the Emperor and the introduction of anti-socialist laws against the SPD.

To gain the full 7 marks you need to mention **what overall effect these policy changes had on the internal affairs of Germany**.

Part (c)

To achieve high marks, you must produce **a balanced answer** which deals with the strengths and weaknesses of Imperial Germany in 1890.

Following a brief introduction, the first part of your answer must cover the **strengths. Make sure you write a separate paragraph for each strength**. You should include the economic strength of Germany, which had gone through an industrial revolution and rivalled Britain as Europe's major industrial power. Also, Germany was Europe's main military power. The state possessed a democratically elected Reichstag, which contained a wide range of political opinions.

Balanced against these strengths, you should mention **weaknesses** such as the major social strains caused by rapid industrial and social change. These led to the rise of the industrial middle and working classes. These groups demanded more political representation. However, a conservative Prussian elite, whose wealth was based on agriculture, dominated Germany. Also, the political system was dominated by the Emperor. Finally, the army possessed considerable political influence.

You need to end with **a conclusion** where – in the light of what you have written – you opt to either agree or disagree with the view in the question.

OCR Unit 3: 'Europe 1825–1890'

(a) Explain why Prussia was able to dominate the German Empire from 1871. [30 marks]

(b) Assess the success of Bismarck's foreign policy from 1871. [60 marks]

How to score full marks

Part (a)

Start by writing **a brief plan** in which you note down several reasons for Prussian dominance. Then try to place them **in order of importance**. You should start **a new paragraph** for each reason. Reasons you could include are:

- Under the Constitution of 1871 the Emperor, who was King of Prussia, hired and fired the chancellor and government. He was commander-in-chief of the army and could make international treaties.

- The new state was dominated by a conservative Prussian elite of large landowners called Junkers.

- The new Germany was a federal state and Prussia was by far the largest state comprising two-thirds of the Empire.

- Prussia contained considerable industrial wealth in the Ruhr and Upper Silesia.

- The army was dominated by the Prussian officer corps.

Make sure that your **grammar, punctuation and spelling** are good. This will ensure that you get high marks. Watch the spelling of words such as Kaiser, Reichstag, Junker etc.

Part (b)

Organise your answer into **separate paragraphs**, beginning with a brief **introduction** and ending with a **conclusion** which offers your overall assessment of Bismarck's foreign policy.

Do not describe. Your whole answer must **assess** Bismarck's policies. You need to provide **judgement** and this must be backed up with **supporting factual evidence**.

You will need to discuss Bismarck's aims of isolating France and maintaining European peace. You should mention that from 1871 to 1890 he did succeed in keeping France isolated. However, his alliance system became increasingly unstable. By 1890, he had signed the Triple Alliance and the Reinsurance Treaty, which were potentially contradictory. Within a few years of Bismarck's fall, the alliance system had collapsed leaving Europe in two armed camps of rival alliances. You should also mention that Bismarck's hope of keeping Austria-Hungary and Russia together in alliance was bound to fail because of their rivalry in the Balkans. On two occasions – in 1877 and 1887 – the Balkans led to the collapse of the Dreikaiserbund.

The quality of your written English will be an important factor in achieving top marks. Make sure you punctuate correctly, using commas, apostrophes etc. where appropriate. Ensure that you spell important words and phrases correctly such as Bismarck and Dreikaiserbund.

Answers to all the 'Questions to try' in this chapter can be found on pages 72–75.

Questions to try

AQA Unit 1 Alternative F: 'Tsarist and Revolutionary Russia 1855–1917'

Study the following source material and then answer the questions that follow.

SOURCE A

Adapted from the petition carried by the marchers on Bloody Sunday, January 1905

We workers, our children and our old, helpless parents have come, Lord, to seek truth and protection from you. We are impoverished and oppressed, unbearable work is imposed on us, we are despised and not recognised as human beings. We are treated as slaves. We have suffered terrible things, but we are pressed ever deeper into the abyss of poverty, ignorance and lack of rights.

SOURCE B

Adapted from a school textbook written in Russia in 1976

The 1905 Revolution was defeated because the workers and peasants did not act in an organised way. The peasants seized land but they were not prepared to rise against the Tsar. Most soldiers remained loyal to the government. The workers themselves did not always act together and with enough determination. The Revolution showed that what was needed was a firm alliance between the workers and peasants that would be led by the Bolshevik Party.

SOURCE C

Adapted from *The End of Imperial Russia 1855–1917* by Peter Waldron, 1997

The October Manifesto declared that the new parliament would be elected on a wider franchise than originally planned and that the Russian people should be granted basic civil rights, including freedom of speech, conscience and assembly. After October 1905 the Tsar increasingly resented that he had been compelled to concede a parliament which limited his autocratic power.

(a) Study Source A.
Using your own knowledge, explain briefly why Russian working people complained about their lives in 1905. [3 marks]

(b) Study Sources B and C and use your own knowledge.
With reference to your own knowledge of the 1905 Revolution, explain how the author of Source C challenges the view put forward in Source B. [7 marks]

(c) Study Sources A, B and C and use your own knowledge.
How important to its survival after 1905 was the willingness of the Tsarist regime to make concessions? [15 marks]

Total marks: 25

How to score full marks

Part (a)

This question asks you to explain briefly, but **make sure you include enough factual information** to score the full 3 marks. **Ensure that you make three separate, credit-worthy statements** to explain why Russian people complained.

Part (b)

Make sure you write in **separate paragraphs** when you cover each Source.

Remember to comment on **the date and provenance of each source** as this will help to explain differences and to highlight bias.

Integrate detailed factual information about the 1905 Revolution with commentary on the two sources.

Part (c)

The **command instruction** asks you to decide '**how important**' the Tsarist regime's willingness to make concessions was as a factor in its survival. **You will have to produce factual evidence to support this claim. You will also need to put forward any alternative views, which suggest that survival was due to other factors**.

Write a short **introduction**, **separate paragraphs** for each factor you cover, and a **conclusion**.

You must **integrate the sources with your own knowledge**. For instance, Source A mentions the need for change; Source B suggests survival was due to division between workers and peasants; while Source C refers to the October Manifesto. However, it also states that Nicholas II resented making concessions. This can be supported by mentioning the increasingly narrow base on which Dumas were elected after 1906.

You should mention the importance of the October Manifesto and the creation of the State Duma. You should also mention Stolypin's social and economic reforms from 1907 to 1911.

To balance your coverage of concessions you should discuss the use of repression.

Study Sources 1–5 below and then answer questions (a)–(c), which follow.

SOURCE 1

From the memoirs of Rodzianko, President of the Duma, referring to the situation in 1915

The Commander-in-Chief stated that he was obliged to stop fighting for lack of ammunition and boots.

'You have influence,' he said. 'Try to get boots for the army.'

I replied that… there were plenty of labour and material in Russia. But one province had leather, another nails, another soles, and still another cheap labour. The best thing to do would be to call a congress of heads of zemstvos and ask their cooperation. The Grand Duke was greatly pleased with this idea.

Realising that there might be objections from the Government, I decided to talk it over separately with some of the Ministers… When I explained… Maklakov said, 'Yes, yes; what you tell me agrees perfectly with the information I get from my agents.'

'What information?'

'That the real object of this meeting is to discuss political questions and demand a constitution.'

SOURCE 2

From a letter written by the Tsarina to the Tsar, 17 November 1916. It was written in response to criticisms made by the Tsar's brother, Grand Duke Nicholas Mikhailovich, of the administration run by the Tsarina and of the influence of Rasputin.

…I read Nickolai's letter and am utterly disgusted… he has always hated me… He is the incarnation of all that is evil, all devoted people loathe him… And you my love, far too good and kind and soft – such a man needs to be held in awe of you… You must back me up, for your own baby's sake. Had we not got Him (Rasputin) all would long have been finished. Let them scream – we must show we have no fear and are firm. Wifey is your staunch One and stands as a rock behind him.

SOURCE 3

A Russian cartoon, published in 1916, showing Rasputin holding the Tsar and Tsarina like puppets.

SOURCE 4

An Okhrana (secret police) report, January 1917

There is a marked increase in hostile feelings among the peasants not only against the government but also against all other social groups. The proletariat of the capital is on the verge of despair. The mass of industrial workers are quite ready to let themselves go to the wildest excesses of a hunger riot. The prohibition of all labour meetings, the closing of trade unions, the prosecution of all men taking an active part in the sick benefits funds, the suspension of labour newspapers, and so on, make the labour masses, led by the more advanced and already revolutionary-minded elements, assume an openly hostile attitude towards the Government and protest with all the means at their disposal against the continuation of the war.

SOURCE 5

From Michael Lynch's *War and Revolution 1914–1917*, published in 1992

What destroyed tsardom was the length of the war. A short war, even if unsuccessful, might have been bearable, as Russia's defeat by Japan 12 years earlier had shown. But the cumulative effect of a long drawn-out struggle proved too destructive to be borne.

(a) Study Source 1.
What can you learn from this source about the reasons for Russia's defeat in the First World War? [3 marks]

(b) Use your own knowledge to explain why the Russian economy was so ill-equipped to cope with the strains of war. [5 marks]

(c) Study Sources 2 and 3.
How far does the evidence in Source 2 support the message of the cartoon (Source 3)?

[5 marks]

(d) Study Sources 3 and 4.
  Assess the value of Sources 3 and 4 to historians enquiring into opposition to the Tsar inside Russia in 1916–17. [5 marks]

(e) Study Sources 4 and 5 and use your own knowledge.
  Do you agree that 'What destroyed tsardom was the length of the war'?
  Explain your answer, using the two sources and your own knowledge. [12 marks]

Total marks: 30

How to score full marks

Part (a)

Make sure you make **three separate, credit-worthy points.**

Part (b)

Make sure you give enough **detailed** factual information. You should **highlight the differences between the long-term and short-term causes** of Russia's economic shortcomings.

Part (c)

You need to compare the sources **by cross-referencing between them**. This will involve quoting relevant extracts from Source 2 and describing aspects of the cartoon (Source 3). To get 5 marks you must state 'how far' one source supports the other source. **It is important that your assessment of 'how far' appears as a separate paragraph at the end of your answer.**

Part (d)

To get the full 5 marks for this question **you must assess the usefulness (utility) of the sources**. To do this, you have to point out **who** produced them, **when** they were produced and **why** they were produced.

Part (e)

You are expected to produce **a balanced answer**. This will involve you in producing **evidence** to support the view that the length of war destroyed tsardom. It will also involve you in providing evidence to suggest it was **other factors**.

You must **integrate your own knowledge** with information from Sources 4 and 5.

To support the view, you should use Source 5, which refers to the length of the war. You should discuss how the length of the war led to major economic problems, such as food shortages and inflation. The length of war also led to the rise in influence of Rasputin and a decline in political stability. The Tsar's decision to take over command of the armed forces personally from 1915 also helped to discredit the Tsar's rule because he was blamed for military defeat.

To offer a counter-balance to this view, you should discuss the social and economic problems associated with Source 4 and the longer-term problems of the regime, which included social, economic and political problems that pre-dated the outbreak of war.

OCR Unit 3: 'Europe 1890–1945 (Russia 1894–1917)'

> **(a)** Explain the extent to which Nicholas II's government introduced political and social reforms in Russia in the period 1906–1914. **[30 marks]**
>
> **(b)** How important a reason for the outbreak of revolution in February 1917 was Russia's involvement in the First World War? **[60 marks]**

How to score full marks

Part (a)

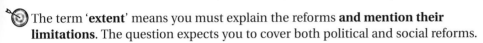 The term '**extent**' means you must explain the reforms **and mention their limitations**. The question expects you to cover both political and social reforms.

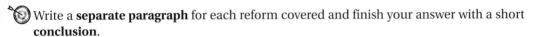 Write a **separate paragraph** for each reform covered and finish your answer with a short **conclusion**.

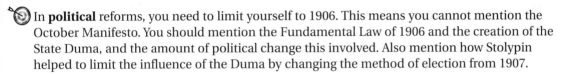 In **political** reforms, you need to limit yourself to 1906. This means you cannot mention the October Manifesto. You should mention the Fundamental Law of 1906 and the creation of the State Duma, and the amount of political change this involved. Also mention how Stolypin helped to limit the influence of the Duma by changing the method of election from 1907.

In **social** reforms, you need to mention Stolypin's social and economic reforms that aided the peasants (e.g. creating the Land Bank and allowing peasants to buy their land). However, you need to mention that virtually nothing was done to help factory workers. This resulted in a new wave of strikes from 1912 to 1914.

Remember – to achieve all 30 marks, not only must your answer include **detailed** factual knowledge but it must be written with **good punctuation, spelling and grammar**.

Part (b)

To achieve full marks you must write a **balanced account – beginning with reasons why the First World War was important** in bringing about the February Revolution, and then moving on to discuss **other factors**. Write out **a BRIEF plan**. Use a separate paragraph for each reason:

> *Paragraph 1:* short introduction
>
> *Paragraph 2:* the economic strains of war; food shortages and inflation
>
> *Paragraph 3:* the Tsar's decision to take control of the army from 1915 made him personally responsible for military defeat.
>
> *Paragraph 4:* the Tsarina, influenced by Rasputin, helped to create political instability at home.
>
> *Paragraphs 5 and 6:* other factors which helped bring about revolution (e.g. long-term problems associated with poor working and living conditions in industrial towns, lack of peasant ownership in the countryside and the lack of political reform).
>
> *Conclusion:* assess 'how important' the war was in the fall of the Tsar. Was it THE most important reason?

Answers to all of the 'Questions to try' in this chapter can be found on pages 75–77.

Questions to try

OCR Unit 3 'Europe 1890–1945: The Causes and Impact of the First World War: 1890–1920'

(a) Identify and explain two consequences of the First World War for the civilian population of Germany during the period 1914 to 1918. [30 marks]

(b) Why was the stalemate of the First World War broken in 1918? [60 marks]

Total marks: 90

How to score full marks

Part (a)

The question requires you to explain **two** consequences of the war for civilians. You will need to **organise your answer so that you offer approximately equal coverage of the two consequences**. If you spend too much time on one, you will not score high marks, however good your explanation is.

You could cover political, cultural, economic or social factors. I suggest you cover one **political consequence**: the German Revolution of 1918, which saw the fall of the Kaiser and the creation of a democratic republic. You will need to explain why this was an important consequence.

You could then write about **the economic consequence** of the war, which was the severe food shortages due to the Allied blockade. This led to the Turnip Winter of 1915–16 and food riots from 1916.

To ensure that you achieve 30 marks you must organise your answer into paragraphs and **write in a good standard of English**.

Part (b)

The command instruction '**why**' requires you **to offer reasons** for the end of the stalemate in 1918. These should include the effects of the Allied blockade, the impact of the US entry into the war, the failure of the German March Offensive at the Second Battle of the Marne and the collapse of Germany's allies such as Turkey and Austria-Hungary.

Remember to place these factors in order of importance.

To score high marks **you need to explain clearly why you regard one of these factors to be the most important**. This can be covered in your **conclusion**.

Study the following sources and then answer the questions that follow.

SOURCE A

Adapted from *The Lost Peace* by Anthony Adamthwaite, 1980

Before 1914 political, economic and demographic forces were eroding Europe's primacy; but the First World War accelerated the process. Japan was now admitted to the ranks of the leading great powers. After 1918 Britain, France and Germany became major debtors to the USA. The war speeded up the winds of nationalist revolt against European colonial rule.

SOURCE B

Adapted from *Europe since Napoleon* by D. Thomson, 1957

The Paris Peace Treaty must stand in history as a conspicuous failure. It was to end by making the worst of both worlds, and to frame a settlement which alienated the vanquished whilst leaving them free and powerful enough to lay immediate plans to destroy it.

SOURCE C

Adapted from *Versailles and After* by Ruth Henig, 1988

The settlement that emerged from the months of deliberation at Versailles was a credible achievement. The fact that it did not survive the 1920s stemmed not so much from the terms of the peace treaties themselves but from the reluctance of the political leaders in the inter-war period to enforce them.

(a) Study Source A and use your own knowledge.
With reference to Source A and to your own knowledge, explain briefly the importance of economic factors before 1918 in the decline of the major European powers.   [3 marks]

(b) Study Sources B and C and use your own knowledge.
With reference to your own knowledge explain how the author of Source C challenges the view of the Versailles settlement put forward in Source B.   [7 marks]

(c) Study Sources A, B and C and use your own knowledge.
How important was the First World War and the treaties which followed it in 'eroding Europe's primacy' in the world?
Your answer should cover the period 1900–1929.   [15 marks]

Total marks: 25

How to score full marks

Part (a)

 To score the full three marks **you need to make three separate, credit-worthy points**. Make sure you **integrate** information from the source with other factual information.

Part (b)

 Firstly, decide what argument each source is putting forward and **summarise it**. For example, 'Source B suggests that the failure of the Paris Peace Treaty was due to the continuance of a powerful, resentful Germany'. Then **introduce factual information that would support this view**. For instance, the 'stab in the back' theory in Germany and the continued belief there that they had not lost the war militarily. Then do the same for Source C, in a separate paragraph.

Part (c)

 To score high marks, you must **organise your answer into a BALANCED account**. You must mention why the First World War and the treaties that followed it helped lead to a decline in Europe's world position. You need to **integrate** source material with your own knowledge. For instance, Source A suggests decline had already started by 1914. The war merely accelerated it. Source B suggests that the treaties created international tension after 1919, which helped the decline of the European powers. This is supported by Source C but for different reasons. This time it was because European politicians were reluctant to enforce the treaties.

 You need to support information from the sources with your own knowledge. For example, the war led to rebellion in Ireland and encouraged the Home Rule movement in India. Both helped to undermine the British Empire. The war also saw the collapse of four European empires: Germany, Russia, Turkey and Austria-Hungary. Finally, the war had a devastating effect on France both in damage and loss of life.

 To balance these views, you need to explain how the growth of the USA and Japan, even before 1914, had begun to challenge the dominant position of Europe in the world.

 Remember to organise your answer into **separate paragraphs for each point made**. Write a short introduction and **a conclusion which mentions 'how important the war and treaties' were to European decline**.

OCR Unit 3: 'Europe and the World 1919–1989'
'International Relations 1919–1939'

(a) Explain the aims of the peacemakers after the First World War. [30 marks]

(b) Compare the responsibility of Britain, France and Germany for the outbreak of the Second World War in 1939. [60 marks]

Total marks: 90

How to score full marks

Part (a)

To achieve high marks you must organise your answer effectively. It must be **divided into paragraphs, each one covering a different aim**. You must include **detailed supporting factual evidence**. Merely mentioning the aims of the peacemakers is not enough. You must explain **why** they had these aims.

You need to discuss why France under Clemenceau wanted to cripple Germany militarily and force Germany to accept heavy reparations and a demilitarised zone in the Rhineland. Reference to the great loss of life and damage to French territory is important.

In dealing with Britain's aims you need to discuss the reasons why Britain wanted to destroy Germany's fleet and claim reparations for war pensions. However, Lloyd George feared the growth of communism and didn't want to weaken Germany too much.

In contrast, Woodrow Wilson of the USA wanted to prevent future wars through the application of national self-determination and the creation of a League of Nations.

Part (b)

The question requires a comparison so do NOT deal with each country in turn. You need to make it clear to the examiner that you can compare. **It would be best to deal with Britain and France together**. You can then assess their responsibility for the outbreak of war through their support for appeasement. References to the demilitarisation of the Rhineland in 1936, the Anschluss in 1938 and, above all, the Czech crisis of 1938 provide ample evidence to support a view that both countries helped cause the war by not supporting the treaties of 1919.

You then need to deal with the role of Hitler and his aims of uniting all Germans and creating 'living space' (Lebensraum) in the East with the destruction of the USSR.

Make sure that you refer constantly to the issue of responsibility for causing the war. Do not write a narrative. You must **use detailed factual evidence** to support your assessment of responsibility.

Finish with **a conclusion** that assesses the responsibility of Britain and France versus Germany.

To achieve the full 60 marks:

- Assess and compare; do not write a narrative.

- Organise your answer into paragraphs.

- Support your assessment with detailed factual evidence.

- Write in a good standard of English.

Answers to all the 'Questions to try' in this chapter can be found on pages 78–80.

Questions to try

Edexcel Unit 2: 'The Triumph of Bolshevism? Russia 1918–1929'

(a) What measures did the Bolsheviks adopt to maintain control of Russia from the revolution of November 1917 to the death of Lenin? **[15 marks]**

(b) Why did Stalin emerge as Lenin's successor after 1924? **[15 marks]**

Total marks: 30

How to score full marks

Part (a)

This question requires you to provide **detailed factual knowledge** of the measures used by the Bolsheviks. **Start by making a BRIEF PLAN**. Note down all the issues you want to cover. For example:

- the ending of Russian participation in the First World War
- dissolving the Constituent Assembly
- keeping political power through terror and repression
- defeating opposition in the Russian Civil War
- introducing the NEP to prevent economic collapse in 1921.

To make sure you get full marks, you must make clear **why** each of these measures was introduced and the effects they had on Bolshevik rule.

Write about each issue in **a separate paragraph** but **try to make links between these issues**. For example, introducing repression and terror helped the Bolsheviks keep political power and aided their victory in the civil war.

Part (b)

Again, **write a brief plan** of the issues you want to cover. For example:

- Amassing widespread control of parts of the government and Communist Party bureaucracy.
- Mention specifically Stalin becoming General Secretary of the Communist Party in 1922.

- Fear of Trotsky, which led to the formation of the Triumvirate of Stalin, Zinoviev and Kamenev.

- The debate about permanent World Revolution and Socialism in One Country.

- The defeat of Zinoviev and Kamenev by Stalin and the Right Opposition on the issue of industrialisation versus continuing the NEP.

- The defeat of the Right Opposition by abandoning the NEP in 1928–29.

It is important that you **place these issues in order of importance**. Mention this in the paragraph on the issue and, again, in the concluding paragraph. If you regard the amassing of bureaucratic power as the most important reason why Stalin emerged as leader of the USSR you will have to explain **why**. This will involve providing **detailed factual evidence to support your case**.

It is important to find links between reasons. For instance, it was Stalin's control of party membership which enabled him to defeat his opponents.

You will need to **deal with each reason in a separate paragraph**. Also, make sure you write a short introduction and a **concluding paragraph**.

Q2

(a) What steps did the communists take in order to solve Russia's economic problems in the years 1921 to 1929? [15 marks]

(b) Why, in the years 1921 to 1929, did communist economic policies change so much? [15 marks]

Total marks: 30

How to score full marks

Part (a)

You must explain what the problems were. You need to refer to:

- economic backwardness

- famine in 1921–22

- collapse of industrial output after First World War

- 80% of Russians were peasants owning small farms

- need to build a strong industrial state in order to spread communism.

Once you have explained the economic problems, you need to mention the specific policies the communists introduced. You will need to mention that between 1918 and 1921 they introduced War Communism. This was followed by the New Economic Policy of 1921–28. In 1928 the rapid planned industrialisation of the USSR was introduced through the Five Year Plan. Also in this policy was the forced collectivisation of Soviet agriculture.

Part (b)

To score high marks, you must place the reasons for the changes in economic policies in what you believe to be their **order of importance**.

You need to find **links between reasons**. You should point out that War Communism came to an end with the conclusion of the Civil War and in response to the Kronstadt Mutiny of 1921. You need to mention the shortcomings of the NEP and how NEPmen benefited from its policies. Also, point out why communists wished to create a modern, industrial state with a large working class, thus destroying a state based on privately-owned, small-scale farms. You could link this to the debate within the Communist Party between socialism in one country, which was supported by Stalin, and permanent world revolution, which was supported by Trotsky.

Don't forget – it is important to write a short introduction and **a concluding paragraph which contains the main reasons for change**.

AQA Alternative F: 'Russia and the USSR 1855–1991'

Unit 3 Revolutionary Russia 1917–1929
Option B: Stalin's Rise to Power 1922–1929

Why did Stalin rather than Trotsky become leader of the Soviet Union? [30 marks]

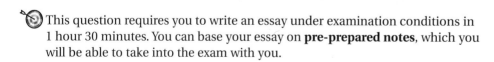

How to score full marks

This question requires you to write an essay under examination conditions in 1 hour 30 minutes. You can base your essay on **pre-prepared notes**, which you will be able to take into the exam with you.

The command instruction '**why**' requires you to give **detailed reasons** for the rise of Stalin to the position of leader. However, you must also give sufficient coverage to **the reasons why Trotsky did not become leader**.

You will probably find it easiest to **start with the reasons why Stalin became leader**. These should include:

- Stalin's acquisition of power through holding posts such as General Secretary of the Communist Party.

- The ability of Zinoviev, Kamenev and Stalin – the Triumvirate – to force Trotsky out of the Politburo.

- The ability of Stalin to win the debate about Socialism in One Country versus Permanent World Revolution.

- Stalin's defeat of Kamenev and Zinoviev in 1926 with the support of Bukharin and Rykov and the Right Opposition.

- Stalin's defeat of Bukharin and Rykov through his support for forced industrialisation from 1928.

You should then go on to discuss **reasons why Trotsky failed to be leader**, including:

- Trotsky's arrogance

- fear of Trotsky as a potential military dictator of the Napoleon type

- Trotsky's late arrival in Bolshevik ranks in 1917

- the unfortunate incapacitation of Lenin when he and Trotsky were planning to remove Stalin.

Your answer should begin with **an introduction**, which explains what you are going to discuss. Try to limit the introduction to two or three sentences.

Use a **separate paragraph for each reason** and ensure that you **place the reasons in order of importance**. Also, try to **find links between reasons**. For instance, Stalin's hold of power within the Communist Party can be linked to his relationship to Kamenev and Zinoviev.

To score high marks, **it is essential that you mention sources that you have used**. Even if you write a good, analytical answer, failure to mention sources will result in you achieving only half marks. If possible, **try to cite a source as evidence for each reason you give** for Stalin's rise and for Trotsky's failure to become leader.

End the essay with a concluding paragraph which provides the main reasons why Stalin, not Trotsky, became leader of the USSR.

AQA Alternative J: 'The Effects of World War 1: 1915–1924'

Option A: The Accession to Power of the Bolsheviks and Lenin's Regime

How much stability had Lenin's regime brought to the USSR by the time of his death?

[30 marks]

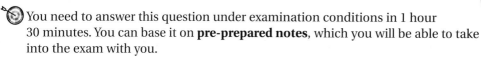 You need to answer this question under examination conditions in 1 hour 30 minutes. You can base it on **pre-prepared notes**, which you will be able to take into the exam with you.

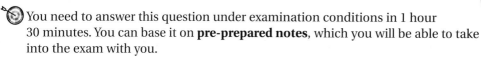 Make sure that in your notes you refer directly to **sources of information**. You will be required to mention specific historians – and what they said – in your answer.

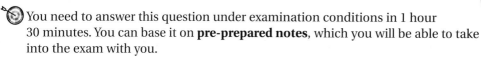 The command instruction '**how much**' indicates that you are expected to provide **an analysis and form a judgement**. You will need to point out areas where Lenin's regime created stability **but you must also provide an evaluation of the level of stability**.

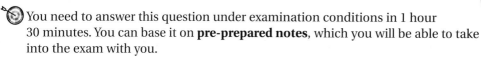 Issues which you need to consider will be:

- political stability
- economic stability
- social stability.

In dealing with **political stability** you need to mention:

- how the Bolsheviks were able to defeat all their opponents in the Civil War
- how they used terror to maintain political control
- how the creation of the USSR, in 1922, helped to solve the problems of different nationalities within the Communist state.

In dealing with **economic stability** you need to mention the economic problems created by Civil War and War Communism, which resulted in a major decline of industrial output and widespread famine by 1921. In contrast, the abandonment of War Communism and the introduction of the NEP brought a degree of economic stability by 1924.

In **social stability** you need to mention that the Communists wanted to create a socialist state based on an industrial working class. Unfortunately, Russia was made up primarily of peasants who owned small farms. If the Communists were to create a socialist state, this situation would have to change.

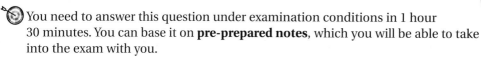 Make sure you begin your answer with **an introduction** which sets out clearly what you plan to discuss. It should not be more than two to three sentences long.

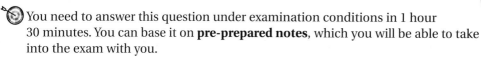 Each point you make must be mentioned in a separate paragraph. **Try to begin your paragraphs with an historical judgement**. This should then by supported by **factual evidence, which should include reference to the sources** from which you got the information.

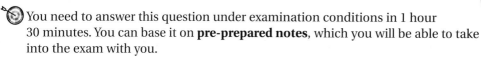 Remember – you must emphasise '**how much**' stability was brought to the Soviet Union **in each point you raise**.

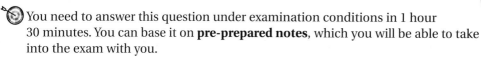 Always end your essay with **a concluding paragraph**, which should mention the main points you have raised in your answer.

Answers to all the 'Questions to try' in this chapter can be found on pages 80–84.

Questions to try

Edexcel Unit 3: 'Life in the Soviet Union 1928–1941'

Study Sources 1 and 2 below and then answer the questions (a)–(c), which follow.

SOURCE 1

Stalin, speaking in 1929

We are advancing full steam ahead along the path of industrialisation – to socialism leaving behind the age-long Russian backwardness. We are becoming a country of metal, a country of automobiles, a country of tractors. And when we have put the USSR on the automobile, and the peasant on the tractor, let the worthy capitalists, who boast so loudly of their civilisation, try to overtake us. We shall see which countries may then be classified as backward and which as advanced.

SOURCE 2

Stalin, speaking in 1931

To slow down the tempo of industrialisation would mean falling behind. And those who fall behind get beaten. The history of old Russia shows that, because of her backwardness, she was continually beaten – because of her military, cultural, political, industrial and agricultural backwardness. We are fifty or hundred years behind the advanced countries. We must make good this distance in ten years. Either we do it or they will crush us.

(a) Study Sources 1 and 2.
   What reasons for industrialisation does Stalin advance in these two sources?   [5 marks]

(b) What contribution did collectivisation of agriculture make to the process of industrialisation?   [7 marks]

(c) Did the lives of the mass of the Russian people improve or worsen as a result of Stalin's economic policies between 1929 and 1941?
   Explain your answer.   [18 marks]

Total marks: 30

How to score full marks

Part (a)

🎯 You may find it easiest to write in separate paragraphs for coverage of Source 1 and coverage of Source 2. This will help to ensure that you do **cover both sources equally**. Candidates often write at length about one source but ignore the other completely, which reduces the marks they can be awarded.

🎯 **Examiners will, however, expect you to make comparisons between the reasons given in the two sources.** These comparisons could be made in the second paragraph of your answer, which deals with Source 2, or could be in a third paragraph.

Part (b)

🎯 This question requires you to **use your own knowledge**. You **must ensure that you make clear links between collectivisation and industrialisation** if you are to get full marks.

Part (c)

🎯 This question requires **analysis and judgement** from you. **You must divide your answer into sections that deal with both sides of the question**.

🎯 Firstly, you will need to **provide evidence that Stalin's economic policies benefited the mass (majority) of the Russian people**. You will need to refer to how industrialisation created thousands of industrial jobs. Also, Stalin's policy of education increased literacy and provided new economic opportunities for most Russians.

🎯 The second section of your answer should **explain how Stalin's economic policies damaged the mass of the Russian people**. Forced collectivisation led to the deaths of millions of peasants. Millions more were forced, against their will, to live on collective farms, forced to move to Siberia or ended up in Gulag concentration camps. Industrialisation also led to considerable misery. Thousands of those who were involved in the Five Year Plans were slave labourers.

🎯 Write a two- or three-sentence **introduction** and then **write a paragraph for each point you raise**. At the end of your essay, make sure you write **a concluding paragraph which states clearly whether or not the mass of the Russian people benefited from Stalin's economic policies**.

OCR Unit 3: 'Europe and the World 1919–1989'

The USSR 1924–1953

(a) Examine the reasons why Stalin became leader of the Soviet Union by 1929. [30 marks]

(b) To what extent did Stalin bring about change in the USSR in the 1930s? [60 marks]

Total marks: 90

How to score full marks

Part (a)

This question requires you to **identify**, and then **explain**, the reasons why Stalin became leader. To achieve full marks you must **avoid writing a narrative chronology of Stalin's rise to power**. Instead, you need **to place the reasons in order of importance**. You need to mention the following issues:

- Stalin's acquisition of bureaucratic power, such as the General Secretaryship of the Communist Party in 1922.

- The untimely death of Lenin, in January 1924, just when Lenin and Trotsky were planning to oust Stalin from the Politburo.

- The dislike and fear of Trotsky by many leading Bolsheviks. They feared Trotsky might become a military dictator.

- The creation of the Triumvirate of Stalin, Kamenev and Zinoviev, which prevented Trotsky becoming leader.

- The debate between socialism in one country and permanent world revolution.

- Stalin's defeat of Kamenev and Zinoviev, in 1926–27, over economic policy.

- Stalin's defeat of Bukharin and the Right Opposition, in 1927–28, over forced industrialisation versus the continuation of the NEP.

You must find **links between reasons**, such as the fear of Trotsky and the creation of the Triumvirate.

Always write a **separate paragraph for each point made**. Remember to write a **concluding paragraph which sums up the main reasons for Stalin's rise**.

Part (b)

The command instruction '**to what extent**' should signal to you that you need **to provide a balanced, analytical answer** which puts forward the case **for and against** the view that Stalin's rule brought about change within the USSR.

You need to begin your answer with **a short introduction**, which sets out what you plan to discuss.

Then you need to **explain the areas where Stalin's rule brought change**:

- Economic change with forced collectivisation and forced industrialisation.

- Political change in the form of creating an absolute dictatorship through the Purges.

- Social change in destroying an independent peasant class that owned small farms.

- The creation of a strong industrial economy with large numbers of Russians now residing in towns.

In **assessing** these changes you will need to state:

- how significant the changes were

- how the changes benefit or damage the USSR.

🎯 The second part of your answer must discuss **the areas where little or no change occurred**:

- The rule by a dictator had been firmly established by 1929.

- The Communist Party's rule had been established before 1930.

- The use of terror through a secret police and the use of the Gulag concentration camp system had already been created before 1930.

🎯 You must include **a conclusion**, which explains clearly **what degree of change had occurred in Russia in the 1930s**.

AQA Unit 1 Alternative J: 'The Origins and Consolidation of Totalitarian Regimes 1918–1939'

Read the following source and then answer the questions that follow.

From *Hope Against Hope* by N. Mandelstam (who lived in the USSR in the 1930s), 1971

My friend Sonia Vishnevski, hearing every day of new arrests among her friends, shouted in horror: 'Treachery and counter-revolution everywhere!' This was how you were supposed to react if you lived in relative comfort and had something to lose.

(a) Explain what was meant by 'counter-revolution' in the USSR in the 1930s. [3 marks]

(b) Explain why Stalin accused so many people of 'treachery and counter-revolution' in the USSR in the 1930s? [7 marks]

(c) Do you agree with the view that Stalin successfully removed 'treachery and counter-revolution' in the USSR in the 1930s? [15 marks]

Total marks: 25

How to score full marks

Part (a)

🎯 To gain full marks you must **explain both the meaning of the term and why it was important in the USSR in the 1930s**.

Part (b)

🎯 Remember to place the reasons why Stalin accused so many people **in order of importance**. This will stop your answer from reading like a random list and will convince the examiner that you have **evaluated the importance of each reason**.

🎯 You will need to write a separate paragraph for each point you mention. Always end your answer with a **brief concluding paragraph** – in this instance, one which **mentions the main reason for Stalin's action**.

Part (c)

This question requires you to produce a **balanced, analytical answer**.

The inverted commas around 'treachery and counter-revolution' are a signal that **you are expected to give a definition of these terms in the context of the 1930s**. These terms applied to anyone who stood in the way of Stalin achieving his aims. For example:

- so-called saboteurs of the Five Year Plan, such as factory managers and economic planners who were blamed for the failure to meet targets

- peasants who opposed collectivisation

- political opponents within the Communist Party

- virtually anyone, by the mid-1930s, whom the secret police – the NKVD – saw as a threat to the State.

The next part of your answer should **discuss the methods Stalin used to deal with those who 'opposed' him**. In this section you should mention political opponents such as Kamenev, Zinoviev and Bukharin, who were all executed in the Great Purge from 1934. You should also include the creation of a terror state where random arrest and imprisonment became the norm by the mid-1930s.

In the final part of your answer you need **to explain why you disagree**, if you do, **with the statement**. For example, you could mention that the forced collectivisation of agriculture led to the deaths of millions in the Ukraine in 1932–33. It also had a very damaging effect on agricultural production. You could also mention that 'Show Trials' of industrial managers, such as the Shakhti Trial (1928), were an excuse for problems within the Five Year Plans rather than a way of dealing with traitors.

Remember to write **a separate paragraph for each point raised** in each part of your answer. Pay attention to the correct spelling of names and historical terms associated with the USSR in the 1930s.

Your answer must end with **a conclusion which sums up whether, on balance, you agree or disagree with the statement**.

Answers to all the 'Questions to try' in this chapter can be found on pages 85–87.

Questions to try

Edexcel Unit 2: 'Italy: The Rise of Fascism 1918–1925'

Q1

(a) Describe the main stages by which fascism developed into an effective political movement between its foundation in March 1919 and the March on Rome in October 1922.

[15 marks]

(b) Why was Mussolini appointed as Prime Minister in 1922?

[15 marks]

Total marks: 30

How to score full marks

Part (a)

Write out **a brief plan** of the points you want to include:

- The reasons for the creation of the Fascist Party in 1919 and its political programme.
- The fear of socialism and communism during the 'Red Year' of 1919.
- The creation of the Fascist squads.
- The leadership crisis of 1921.
- The fascist revolution of 1921–22.
- The alliance with the monarchy and the Catholic Church.

You should **deal with each point in a separate paragraph**, even though some paragraphs will be short. What is important is to **make sure that you make links between each point in the main stages of Fascist development**. For instance, the support of the monarchy and Church should be linked to the fear of socialism and communism.

Part (b)

You must place the reasons for Mussolini's appointment as Prime Minister **in order of importance and find links between them**. You need to mention:

- the weakness of liberal governments and the mistakes they made in 1921–22
- Mussolini's anti-socialism
- Mussolini's support for Italian nationalism
- King Victor Emmanuel III's fear of civil war and socialism
- Pope Pius XI's fear of socialism
- Mussolini's clever tactics associated with the March on Rome in October 1922.

Q2

(a) What opposition did Mussolini face as Prime Minister in the years 1922 to 1924?

[15 marks]

(b) Why did he establish a dictatorship in 1925?

[15 marks]

Total marks: 30

How to score full marks

Part (a)

 In your answer you should include reference to:

- liberal parties in parliament
- the Catholic Populari Party
- socialists and communists, in particular Matteotti
- opponents within the Fascist movement.

Not only must you identify the opponents, **you must say why they opposed Mussolini**.

To achieve full marks make sure you mention **how Mussolini dealt with his critics. This should appear at the end of your answer**.

Remember to **write a separate paragraph** for each set of opponents you identify.

Part (b)

You should mention:

- Fascism was a set of political ideas that were anti-democratic and would eventually lead to dictatorship.
- Mussolini was able to establish effective control over the Fascist movement by 1925, in particular in dealing with local Fascist leaders, the Ras.
- Mussolini was able to get the Acerbo Law passed through parliament, which gave Fascists effective control after the 1923 election.
- The Matteotti Affair led to the Aventine Succession of Mussolini's political opponents in parliament, which gave the Fascists complete control by 1925.

It is important that you attach a degree of importance to each of the issues raised above. **Also, make links between reasons** – for instance, the Matteotti Affair and the Aventine Succession.

Your answer must end with **a concluding paragraph, which summarises the reasons you have discussed**.

Italy 1919–1939

(a) Identify and explain the reasons why Mussolini came to power in Italy.　　　[30 marks]

(b) Assess Mussolini's success by 1939 in making Italy a stable and prosperous country.　　　[60 marks]

Total marks: 90

How to score full marks

Part (a)

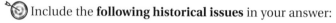Include the **following historical issues** in your answer:

- the weakness of Italian democracy and instability of governments
- fear of socialism and communism
- the effectiveness of Fascist squads in dealing with opponents
- Mussolini's support for nationalism and traditional political elites
- the events surrounding the March on Rome in October 1922
- the reasons why Mussolini was appointed Prime Minister by the King.

To achieve high marks, you must explain which were long-term causes, short-term causes and the immediate cause. Also, it is important to place these reasons in an order of importance.

Part (b)

The command word '**assess**' signals that your answer must be **a balanced one, which provides evidence for and against** the view that Mussolini created a stable and prosperous country by 1939.

Make sure you offer **a brief explanation of the terms 'stable' and 'prosperous' in the context of Italy in the 1930s**. It is probably easiest to do this in your short introduction.

In **support** of the view that Mussolini brought stability and prosperity you need to discuss:

- the creation of a dictatorship
- the use of propaganda to create the image of political stability
- the use of the secret police to silence political opponents.

You could also mention the Lateran Treaties with the Pope and the building of roads and public buildings.

In **opposition** to the view that Mussolini brought stability you should discuss how stability was bought at a cost – which was political repression. With regard to prosperity, you should mention that many of Mussolini's economic policies were not successful, such as Quota 90 and the battle for grain. Italy suffered from the impact of economic depression after 1929.

 Remember, your answer must end with **a conclusion**, which provides **your own judgement on whether or not Mussolini was successful in creating stability and prosperity**.

AQA Unit 1 Alternative J: 'The Origins and Consolidation of Totalitarian Dictatorships 1918–1939'

Read the following source and then answer the questions that follow.

From *The European Dictatorships 1918–1945* by Stephen J. Lee, 1987

Almost all the great personalities of the [inter-war] period were critics of democracy. The masses were tempted by their charisma, sweeping promises and simple solutions.

(a) What was meant by 'critics of democracy' in relation to the rise of inter-war totalitarian regimes? [3 marks]

(b) Explain why the one-party state was established in the inter-war period in Italy. [7 marks]

(c) 'The role of the individual leader was the most important factor in the development of the one-party state in the period 1922 to 1939.'
With reference to Italy, explain why you agree or disagree with this statement. [15 marks]

Total marks: 25

How to score full marks

Part (a)

 This part is worth 3 marks so make sure you make **at least three credit-worthy points**. You need to place the term in **a wider context than just Italy**.

Part (b)

 You must explain **why** Mussolini became Prime Minister in October 1922 and **how he created a dictatorship** by 1925. Your answer should include the following points:

● Fascism was anti-democratic and a one-party state was a major political aim of Mussolini.

● The weaknesses and mistakes of liberal politicians and governments.

● The King appointed Mussolini Prime Minister in October 1922 because he feared a civil war and preferred fascism to socialism and communism.

- The Acerbo Law of 1923 gave the Fascists control of parliament after the 1923 elections.
- The Matteotti Affair and the Aventine Succession gave the Fascists control over parliament, which allowed them to ban other political parties.

You must place these points **in an order of importance with a brief explanation why you regard some factors as more important than others**.

Your answer must be divided up into paragraphs where **each point mentioned above is dealt with in a separate paragraph**.

Part (c)

This question requires you to provide **a balanced, analytical answer** where you **assess the importance of the role of Mussolini against other reasons** for the creation of a one-party state in Italy from 1922 to 1939.

Your answer should begin with **a brief introduction**, which sets out what you plan to explain in your answer.

The first part of your answer must deal with the importance of Mussolini in creating one-party rule in Italy. You should mention:

- Mussolini's personal qualities as an orator.
- The use of propaganda which portrayed Mussolini as Il Duce, the leader of the nation.
- The ability of Mussolini as a politician in passing the Acerbo Law and in dealing with the Matteotti Affair.

In the second half of your answer you need to assess other factors, such as:

- the weakness and divisions amongst political opponents
- the dictatorial, anti-democratic nature of Fascism
- the use of the secret police, OVRA, to silence political opponents.

Remember to write in **separate paragraphs for each point** you make.

You must write **a concluding paragraph** which assesses the importance of the role of Mussolini. From the evidence you produce in your answer you must state **whether or not it was the most important factor**. If not, you must state **which factor was more important – with a brief explanation why**.

Answers to all the 'Questions to try' in this chapter can be found on pages 87–90.

Questions to try

Edexcel Unit 1: 'The Seeds of Evil: The Rise of National Socialism in Germany to 1933'

Study Sources 1–5 below and then answer the question (a)–(e) that follow.

SOURCE 1

From Goebbel's Diary

<u>30 May 1932</u>   The bomb has exploded. Bruning has presented the resignation of the entire Cabinet to the President at noon. The system has begun to crumble. The President has accepted the resignation. I at once ring up the Fuhrer. Now he must return to Berlin at once ...

Meet the Fuhrer at Nauern. The President wishes to see him in the course of the afternoon. We are delighted.

The conference with the President went off well. The SA prohibition is going to be cancelled. Uniforms are going to be allowed again. The Reichstag is going to be dissolved. That is of the first importance.

Von Papen is likely to be appointed Chancellor but that is neither here nor there. The poll! The poll! It is the people we want. We are entirely satisfied.

SOURCE 2

From the monthly magazine of the NSDAP propaganda department, July 1931

The preparation of the village meeting is carried out most effectively by sending written personal invitations to every farmer or inhabitant. In the bigger villages a circular should be carried from farm to farm by party comrades. At the meeting itself the question of finance has to be considered. Our movement is so poor that every penny counts. Collections must therefore be held during all discussion evenings and also in the big mass meetings if permitted by the police, either in the interval or at the end, even when the entrance fee has been taken at the beginning of the meeting. In this way, especially when plates and not a cup is used, surprising amounts can sometimes be got out of a meeting.

SOURCE 3

An anti-NSDAP cartoon entitled 'Millions stand behind me', 1932. It shows Hitler dependent on big business.

SOURCE 4

Number of seats won and percentage of votes cast in favour of the NSDAP in the elections of 1932.

Reichstag elections	July	November
Number of seats	230	196
National vote (%)	37.3	33.1
Selected districts:		
East Prussia (rural East Germany)	47.1	39.7
Berlin (capital city)	24.6	22.5
Schleswig-Holstein (rural north)	51.0	45.7
Cologne-Aachen (industrial W. Germany)	20.2	17.4
Dusseldorf (industrial W. Germany)	31.6	27.0
Lower Bavaria (southern Germany)	20.4	18.5

SOURCE 5

From *The Nazi Voter*, by Thomas Childers 1985

If the party's support was a mile wide, it was at critical points an inch deep. The NSDAP had managed to build a remarkably varied support, overcoming regional divisions, linking town and country, and spanning the social divides, and shrinking the gap between religious groupings in Germany. Yet the basis of that extraordinary electoral alliance was dissatisfaction, resentment and fear. It therefore remains one of history's most tragic ironies that at precisely the moment when the movement's electoral support had begun to falter, Hitler was installed as Chancellor by representatives of those traditional elites who had done so much to undermine the parliamentary system in Germany.

(a) Study Source 1.
What does this source reveal about the reason for Goebbel's optimism in May 1932?

[3 marks]

(b) Use your own knowledge to explain the role and importance of the SA in building Nazi support before January 1933.

[5 marks]

(c) Study Sources 4 and 5.
How far does Source 4 support the statement in Source 5 that 'the NSDAP had managed to build a remarkably varied support'?

[5 marks]

(d) Study Sources 2 and 3.
Compare the value of these two sources to an historian studying the funding of the NSDAP in 1932.

[5 marks]

(e) Study Sources 1 and 5 and use your own knowledge.
Do you agree that the role played by the traditional elites was the main factor bringing Hitler to power in January 1933?
Explain your answer, using these two sources and your own knowledge.

[12 marks]

Total marks: 30

How to score full marks

Part (a)

This question requires you to use information from the source and **place it in historical context**. Remember this question is worth 3 marks so you should write **more than a paragraph**. From the source you should mention that Goebbels is optimistic because a Reichstag election is to be held and the ban on the SA is to be lifted by President Hindenburg. This would provide an opportunity for the Nazis to win more electoral support. It is important **to quote from the source** in support of your answer.

Part (b)

This question requires you to use your own knowledge. You are asked two questions:

- What was **the role** of the SA?

- What was **its importance**?

You should ensure that both parts of the question are in your answer.

To make sure you get full marks you need to mention precisely how the SA helped the Nazis gain votes at the expense of other parties up to January 1933 when Hitler was appointed Chancellor. It would be useful if you wrote **two paragraphs**, each dealing with a different aspect of the question.

Part (c)

To score full marks on this question **you must cross-reference between the two sources**. Do not deal with the sources separately. Also, you need to explain '**how far**' they are in agreement as this is specifically called for by the wording of the question.

You need to study Source 4 and use information from it to explain what Thomas Childers states in Source 5. You should refer to the **varied support of the Nazis** overcoming regional divisions. You should also mention how the Nazis received votes in **both** Protestant (north) and Catholic (south) Germany.

Make sure, however, that you **spot differences between the sources**. For example, Source 4 highlights that the Nazis did best in rural areas, which does not fully support the claim of 'remarkably varied support' in Source 5.

Part (d)

To get full marks you must refer **both to the authorship and the content of both sources**. Source 2 is from a pro-Nazi source; Source 3 is from an anti-Nazi source. You need to say whether the source content is full of **factual information or opinion**. Source 2 is mainly factual; Source 3 is an opinion. Finally, you need to mention **the motive behind the production of both sources**. Remember that your answer must clearly **compare the value of each source to an historian**.

Part (e)

Remember to follow the instructions closely. You must use Source 1, Source 5 and your own knowledge.

You are also expected to produce **a balanced answer**. Firstly, you must explain the importance of the role of traditional elites in bringing Hitler to power. Then you need to mention other factors that brought him to power. **For each factor you should write a separate paragraph**.

In Source 1 you can use evidence of how Hindenburg helped the Nazis by calling an election and lifting the ban on the SA. This is supported in the final part of Source 5, which states that Hitler was made Chancellor because traditional elites had undermined the parliamentary system. But you need **to include other factors** such as the economic depression, Hitler's programme, the role of the SA, fear of communism and the weakness of other right-wing parties.

It is important to write **a concluding paragraph in which you assess whether or not the role of traditional elites was the MAIN factor**. It does not matter whether you agree or disagree as long as you provide **clear evidence to support your view**.

Read the following source and then answer the questions that follow.

Adapted from *The Weimar Republic* by J. Hiden, 1974

The Versailles Treaty certainly did not doom the Republic from birth, but it did make existing internal conflicts much worse.

(a) What was meant by 'existing internal conflicts' in the context of Germany in early 1919? [3 marks]

(b) Explain why the Versailles Treaty provoked outrage in Germany. [7 marks]

(c) 'Right-wing opposition was the main cause of the difficulties of the Weimar Republic to 1925.'
Explain why you agree or disagree with this view. [15 marks]

Total marks: 25

How to score full marks

Part (a)

As this question is worth 3 marks write **one paragraph**. You need to limit your answer to early 1919. Therefore, you will need to mention the Spartacist Uprising in Berlin and the socialist takeover in Bavaria.

Part (b)

In this question you must use **your own knowledge**. Write a **short, separate paragraph for each main point you raise**. You need to mention the 'War Guilt' clause (231) and reparations (article 232); the loss of colonies and lands in Europe, in particular the Polish Corridor which split Germany in two. You also need to mention German disarmament and the demilitarisation of the Rhineland.

Part (c)

This question is worth over half the total marks. You need to write **a short essay that puts forward a balanced assessment**.

The first part of your answer must **provide evidence of right-wing opposition to the Weimar Republic**. You should mention the Kapp Putsch of March 1920, the assassinations of Erzberger and Rathenau by right-wing groups and the Beer Hall Putsch of 23 November.

In the second part of your answer you need **to mention other difficulties** such as left-wing opposition in the Spartacist uprising and the Red Revolution in the Ruhr and Saxony in 1920. However, you also need to mention the hyper-inflation of 1922 and 1924 and the Franco–Belgian occupation of the Ruhr in 1923–24.

You must write **a concluding paragraph** where, based on the evidence you have produced, you mention **whether or not right-wing opposition was the MAIN difficulty**.

Europe 1890–1945: 4 Germany 1919–1945

The first part of this unit deals with the Weimar Republic.

Either

(a) How serious were the economic problems facing the Weimar Republic?   [30 marks]

Or

(b) Explain why the Nazi Party grew in popularity between 1930 and 1933.   [30 marks]

How to score full marks

Part (a)

- In your answer you need **to identify the different periods of economic crisis faced by the Weimar Republic**. You need to mention that 1919–1924 was a period of economic difficulties associated with the dislocation caused by the war and reparations. It led to hyper-inflation by 1922 to 1924. However, although serious, the Republic survived as a result of the Dawes Plan and the introduction of the Rentenmark.

- You also need to mention that the period 1925 to 1929 was a **period of relative prosperity** for the Republic.

- Finally, you need to mention that the 1929–33 **economic crisis** was very serious and led to the collapse of the Republic with the appointment of Hitler. Remember: the 1929–33 crisis was associated with mass unemployment and falling prices, not inflation.

- To score full marks, you need to make **a direct reference to 'how serious' the economic difficulties were**.

Part (b)

- This question requires you to provide **reasons** for the rise in popularity of the Nazi Party between 1930 and 1933. Divide your answer into **separate paragraphs**, each dealing with reasons why the Nazis became popular. You need to consider the following in your answer:

    (i) the economic crisis

    (ii) fear of communism

    (iii) popularity of Nazi policies

    (iv) use of the SA.

- In your **conclusion**, it is important to mention what you regard as **the MAIN reason**.

Answers to all the 'Questions to try' in this chapter can be found on pages 90–92.

Questions to try

AQA Unit 1 Alternative L: 'US Foreign Policy 1890–1991'

Read the following and then answer the questions which follow.

> **From *America in the Twentieth Century* by James Patterson, 1999**
>
> Truman's anti-communism led him deliberately to exaggerate the Soviet threat. This was the approach that he used in 1947 in getting Congress to approve the Truman Doctrine.

(a) What was meant by 'the Truman Doctrine' in relation to US foreign policy during the Cold War in Europe after 1945? [3 marks]

(b) Explain how Truman dealt with the Soviet blockade of Berlin in the years 1948–49. [7 marks]

(c) Do you agree or disagree with the view that Truman's Administration was successful in its relations with the Soviet Union in respect to European affairs between 1945 and 1949?
Explain your answer. [15 marks]

Total marks: 25

How to score full marks

Part (a)

You will need to **write a paragraph** explaining what the Truman Doctrine was and why it was introduced. You will need to mention the policy of containment and why Truman wanted to introduce it in 1947 following Britain's inability to defend Greece during the Greek Civil War.

Part (b)

To gain full marks, **you must give a full explanation** of how Truman used the Berlin Airlift to overcome the Soviet blockade of west Berlin. **Avoid writing a narrative.** You need to explain that Truman's options were limited in how he could supply west Berlin. Also, this was a major test for the policy of containment and Truman had to show the world that the USA was determined to defend west Berlin.

Part (c)

To score full marks **you need to produce a balanced answer** in which you first deal with Truman's successes and then areas where he was not successful. In providing evidence of success you need to mention:

- the Truman Doctrine and the Marshall Plan of 1947
- the defeat of the communists in the Greek Civil War
- the Berlin Airlift crisis of 1948–49
- and the creation of NATO in 1949.

To **balance these successes** you need to mention the Soviet takeover of eastern Europe. In particular, you need to mention the takeover of Czechoslovakia in 1948.

You need to produce **a concluding paragraph** that mentions whether or not, on the basis of the evidence you have produced in your answer, you agree or disagree with the view put forward in the questions.

OCR Unit 3: 'Europe and the World 1919–1989'

3 The Cold War in Europe 1945–1989

(a) Explain why the alliance against Nazi Germany collapsed so soon after the end of the Second World War. [30 marks]

(b) By what means, and how successfully, did the USSR maintain control over the other eastern European states during the period 1945–1989? [60 marks]

Total marks: 90

How to score full marks

Part (a)

To score full marks **you must give a number of clear reasons**. The question refers to 'soon after' the end of the Second World War so you should not go beyond 1947.

Make sure you write **a separate paragraph for each major reason you give**. Also, it is important to **place the reasons in an ORDER OF IMPORTANCE**. The reasons you should consider are:

- differences in ideology between democracy and communism
- the hostility between Truman and Stalin
- the Soviet takeover of eastern Europe
- Soviet fear of US nuclear weapons.

- You must make sure you deal with both parts of the question: **'by what means'** and **'how successfully'**.

- You will need to write your answer in **separate paragraphs**. You will also have to cover the whole period in your answer, from 1945 to 1989.

- In dealing with '**by what means**', you will need to mention the use of the Red Army, the creation of communist government across eastern Europe, and the building of the Berlin Wall in 1961. In dealing with '**how successfully**', it is clear that the USSR was successful up to 1989 in maintaining communist control. However, you need to mention developments such as the East German Revolt of 1953, the Hungarian Uprising of 1956 and the Polish Solidarity problem of 1981–82.

---

4 The Cold War in Asia and the Americas 1949–1975

(a) How dangerous to international peace was the Cuban Missile Crisis?

[30 marks]

(b) Compare the importance of at least **three** factors that contributed to the failure of the USA to win the Vietnam War.

[60 marks]

Total marks: 90

How to score full marks

Part (a)

- You need to address the issue of 'how dangerous' in your answer. **Avoid writing a narrative**. Instead, you need to explain why the crisis almost led to nuclear war between the superpowers. **Write a separate paragraph for each reason**. You need to write about:

  - the proximity of Cuba to the USA and the threat of medium-range nuclear missiles to America;

  - the decision by Kennedy to quarantine the island leading to a direct confrontation with the USSR.

- All of these developments need to be placed **within the context of the Cold War and nuclear arms race between the two superpowers by 1962**. The crisis was serious because the USA reached 'Defcon 2', one step before launching all-out nuclear war. The aftermath of the crisis reflected its danger because both superpowers signed the Test Ban Treaty of 1963 and established the Molink between the White House and the Kremlin.

Part (b)

First, you need to **identify three factors** that contributed to US failure in the Vietnam War. These should be:

(i) the effective use of guerrilla tactics by the Vietcong and North Vietnamese

(ii) opposition to the war within the USA

(iii) the ineffective nature of US military tactics.

Once you have identified these factors, **you must compare their importance** if you are to score full marks. **This means placing them in an order of importance. You also need to link them**. The guerrilla tactics of the communists were not met effectively by US tactics of search and destroy or aerial bombing and use of Agent Orange. US military tactics were heavily criticised within the USA and undermined the ability of the United States to fight the war. You need to mention the My Lai massacre, use of Agent Orange and napalm, and attacks on civilians which were televised in the USA.

Answers to all the 'Questions to try' in this chapter can be found on pages 93–95.

2 The unification of Germany 1850–1871

How to score full marks

AQA Unit 1 Alternative G: 'Imperial and Weimar Germany 1866–1925'

(a) The illustration depicts Bismarck as a blacksmith, which relates to the idea that he was known as the 'Iron Chancellor'. It attempts to show that Bismarck, more than any other individual, was responsible for the creation of a united Germany under Prussia. In the war against Austria, in 1866, and in the war against France, in 1870–71, Bismarck transformed Prussia from the main north German state into the German Empire.

(b) Source C challenges the view in Source B because it offers criticism of Bismarck's intentions and methods. Source B, written by Erich Eyck portrays Bismarck as a great statesman. He regards Bismarck as having 'courage and patience' and had 'never failing skill'. He gives the strong impression that Bismarck was the man responsible for the strength and power of the German Empire at the end of the 19th century.

Source C views Bismarck differently. Norman Davies, like Erich Eyck, recognises that Bismarck was a master of politics. However, he points out that Bismarck's tactics were undemocratic and aggressive. Davies accepts that Bismarck was responsible for creating a strong German Empire. However, this German Empire was undemocratic. Although a democratically elected Reichstag existed, it had little power. Political power was mainly in the hands of the German Emperor and the conservative Junker class of large landowners from Prussia.

Source B seems to offer only a one-sided interpretation of Bismarck. Source C accepts Bismarck's great political skill but also recognises that the German Empire he created was conservative and aggressive in foreign affairs.

(c) Between 1866 and 1871, Bismarck played a very important role in the unification of Germany. However, it is important to compare Bismarck's role against other factors.

As Source A suggests, Bismarck was the man who helped forge the German Empire in successful wars against Austria, in 1866, and against France, in 1870–71. This view is supported by Source B. Eyck claims that Bismarck's great skills were an important factor. For instance, in 1866 Bismarck made sure Austria fought Prussia without allies. He had made an agreement with Napoleon III and an alliance with Italy. He was also able to make sure that France fought Prussia without allies in 1870.

Source B suggests that Bismarck had the skill to find 'a way out of the most difficult and complicated situations'. This is shown in 1870 when he was able to force France in to a war through the Ems Telegram. It seemed that France had won a great diplomatic victory when it forced William I to withdraw the Hohenzollern candidate to the Spanish throne. However, Bismarck's ability to edit the Ems Telegram was seen in France as insulting and forced Napoleon III and the Ollivier government to declare war on Prussia. The French declaration of war allowed the South German states to join Prussia because of the military alliance Bismarck had signed with them in 1866.

Although Bismarck played a very important role in the unification of Germany, other factors were also important. In 1866 Napoleon III had hoped that the Austro–German War would be long and costly to both sides. He then hoped France would mediate between them and gain territory in western Germany as a result. The swiftness of Prussian victory upset the French. Napoleon III's quest for territory in west Germany and Luxembourg after 1866 raised international tension in Europe. It was the French, in 1870, who declared war on Prussia in reply to the Ems Telegram.

The Prussian army was also an important factor in the unification of Germany. No matter how skilled Bismarck might be as a politician he could not have been successful without the army which was led expertly by von Moltke.

Bismarck was also fortunate that he wanted to create a Prussian-dominated Germany that received widespread support from German nationalists. They were willing to overlook his aggressive, warlike policies, as mentioned in Source C, if he united the German states.

The Prussians were also successful in providing political unity for Germany during a period of rapid industrial development, which helped unite the German states economically.

Overall, Bismarck made the most important contribution to the unification of Germany. However, he was helped by the quality of the Prussian army and the support of German nationalists.

Edexcel Unit 3: 'Bismarck and the Unification of Germany c 1848–1871'

(a) The author of Source 1, John Venedy, criticises Bismarck's methods in a number of ways. He believes that you cannot unite Germany merely by armed might. He states in line 4 that the 'conquest of all Germany would not lead to German unity'.

He also believes that if Germany is to be united it will have to be with 'respect for German law' and 'popular self-government'. The author believes that German unity can only be achieved by consent. He therefore criticises Bismarck's methods of 'blood and iron' which involved wars with Austria in 1866 and France in 1870–71.

(b) Between 1864 and 1866 Bismarck achieved a localised war with Austria for a number of reasons.

Firstly, he made sure that Russia would not take part. Up to 1855 Russia had been part of the Holy Alliance with Prussia and Austria. However, Austria and Russia became enemies during the Crimean War. In 1863 Bismarck made sure Russia would stay neutral in a war between Austria and Prussia by helping the Russians to put down the Polish Revolt.

Secondly, Bismarck made sure France would not take part by secretly meeting Napoleon III at Biarritz. He was able to get Napoleon III to stay neutral in a war with Austria by suggesting that France might receive some territory if Prussia won.

Finally, Bismarck made sure that Italy would not support Austria by signing a secret alliance with it. By the alliance Italy would receive Venetia if Prussia defeated Austria.

By these means, Bismarck made sure that Austria would not have any allies outside Germany when a war broke out in 1866.

(c) There were a number of reasons why Bismarck could not include the Southern States in a united Germany in 1866 but could do so in 1871.

In 1866 Bismarck had just defeated Austria in the Seven Weeks War. At the end of that war he was able to destroy the old German Confederation. He replaced it with the North German Confederation. This was a new organisation dominated by Prussia. This new confederation would take time to develop under Prussian control. Therefore, it would have been difficult to include the South German States who had traditionally been supporters of Austria. They had supported Austria because they were catholic states, unlike Prussia and north Germany which were mainly Protestant. Nevertheless, Bismarck was able to sign a secret military alliance, which meant that the South German States would support Prussia in a future war.

Another reason why these states could not be included in a united Germany was the opposition of France. Napoleon III of France had hoped that the war between Prussia and Austria would be long. Then France could intervene and gain territory. The speed of Prussian victory took Napoleon III by surprise. Napoleon III might have intervened in a war against Prussia if Bismarck had tried to unite with the South German States.

However, by 1871, Bismarck had succeeded in creating a united Germany which included the Southern States. This was mainly due to the war declared by France against Prussia in July 1870. Under the secret military alliance, the Southern States joined Prussia. Together the North German Confederation and the Southern States defeated the French.

In 1871, the Southern States joined Prussia in a united Germany. There were willing to do so because Bismarck allowed them many privileges. He allowed them to keep separate postal services. Bavaria had special treatment by keeping its own army in peacetime and its own railway system.

Therefore, the situation in Germany had changed radically from that in 1866. The Southern States had fought a major war alongside Prussia and had special rights under the Imperial Constitution of 1871.

OCR Unit 2: 'Europe 1825 to 1890'

(a) By 1860 a number of important economic and political factors helped Prussia to increase its influence in Germany.

In economic terms Prussia had increased its influence in Germany through the establishment of a customs union or Zollverein. This union involved all the states of the German Confederation except Austria. As a result, German states looked towards Prussia for leadership in economic matters rather than to Austria.

Prussian economic influence was also increased because of the industrial revolution in Germany, which began about 1850. Prussia contained two very important areas, which became centres for German industry. In the west was the Ruhr valley. This contained large amounts of coal and iron. It was the centre of the German iron and engineering industries. In the east was Upper Silesia. This area also contained iron ore and coal and was rapidly developing into a major industrial area. Prussia also dominated the German railway system. All the major railway lines went through

Prussia. This new form of communication helped Prussia increase its economic influence.

In political matters the failure of the 1848 revolutions had meant that liberals in Frankfurt would not unite Germany. Instead German nationalists looked to either Prussia or Austria to unite Germany. Prussia was aided, in this respect, by having a very well organised army which was the best in Germany.

Unfortunately Austria was a backward country economically. It was also divided into many racial groups. By the 1850s the Hungarians were looking for more freedom and equality within the Empire. This weakened Austria. In 1859 Austria was defeated by France in a war in north Italy. As a result, Austria lost the province of Lombardy.

Therefore, Prussia increased its influence because of major economic developments within Prussia and due to the political weakness and economic backwardness of Austria.

(b) In the achievement of German unity Bismarck's role was very important, but so were a number of other factors.

Bismarck helped King William I of Prussia overcome the constitutional crisis of 1862. This involved a clash between the liberals and the king over the increase in the army. Bismarck took over as Minister-President of Prussia in 1862 and ruled the country without parliament. He provided strong effective leadership, which allowed Prussia to exploit the opportunities that came its way in the 1860s.

In 1863–64 Bismarck was able to use his diplomatic skill to unite with Austria in a war against Denmark over the German duchies of Schleswig-Holstein. Bismarck was able to make sure that Denmark did not have any allies. Also, at the end of the war, he acquired Schleswig for Prussia which gave Bismarck's state a North Sea coastline.

In the war against Austria, in 1866, Bismarck also showed great diplomatic skill. He made sure Austria fought the war without allies. He made

friends with Russia and France. He also signed a secret alliance with Italy to help fight against the Austrians. As a result, Prussia was able to defeat the Austrians in seven weeks. This enabled Prussia to dominate Germany. In the Treaty of Prague, 1866, Austria was removed from German affairs, the German Confederation was abolished and Prussia dominated north Germany.

Bismarck was also able to outwit the French Emperor, Napoleon II, after 1866. France demanded territorial compensation for staying neutral in the war with Austria. Bismarck prevented France from getting territory in the Rhineland and Luxembourg. By 1870, the French were so incensed that they demanded the Prussian candidate to the Spanish throne be withdrawn. Even though the Prussians agreed, Bismarck's editing of the Ems Telegram forced France into a war which Prussia won.

Although Bismarck's role was the most important reason for German unity there were other factors. Both Austria in 1866 and France in 1870 were poorly led. Their armies were ill equipped compared with the Prussian Army.

Bismarck was also helped by the growth of German nationalism. Nationalists supported Bismarck in his wars against Austria and France because it helped unite Germany into one state. In 1870, the South German States were willing to join Prussia and the North German states because they supported German nationalism.

Finally, Bismarck was aided by the development of the German economy. The economy was going through a period of rapid change which brought German states closer together. The economic growth and the development of railways made Prussia a powerful state.

In conclusion, although Bismarck's role was the most important in the creation of a united Germany, other factors, in particular the might of the Prussian army, helped Bismarck.

How to score full marks

AQA Unit 1 Alternative E: 'Germany and Russia before the First World War 1870–1914'

Q1 (a) The Dreikaiserbund was an international agreement between Germany, Austria-Hungary and Russia. It was first signed in 1873 but collapsed during the Balkan crisis of 1875–78. However, it was renewed in a slightly different form from 1881 to 1887. It was important in Bismarck's foreign policy because it was a way in which he wanted to isolate France diplomatically. It also helped Bismarck keep Austria-Hungary and Russia from quarrelling in the Balkans.

(b) The author of Source C differs in his view of Bismarck's foreign policy from the author of Source B for a number of reasons. Firstly, he believes that Bismarck's foreign policy was well planned and had the potential of maintaining European peace and Germany's dominant position in Europe. This differs from Source B where John Lowe believes that Bismarck became involved in the War in Sight crisis of 1875 for 'no good reason and with no clear purpose'. As a result he suggests that not all Bismarck's foreign policy was well planned. The author of Source B also suggests that Bismarck deliberately provoked that crisis threatening rather than preserving peace.

These two historians have different views because John Lowe is referring to one specific crisis, in 1875, while Stephen Lee takes a broader view over the whole of Bismarck's foreign policy.

(c) Bismarck's system of alliances did help maintain European peace to a large extent between 1871 and 1890.

As shown in Source A, Bismarck possessed considerable influence in European affairs. In the Dreikaiserbund of 1873–77 and 1881–87 he helped keep three Great Powers in alliance. This helped to isolate France but also helped keep Austria-Hungary and Russia from creating conflict in the Balkans.

This view is supported by the author of Source C. Stephen Lee claims that Bismarck's alliances maintained European peace. In the period 1871 to 1890, Bismarck used a number of alliances for this purpose. In addition to the Dreikaiserbund he formed a

formal, secret alliance with Austria-Hungary from 1879. This was the Dual Alliance. It was enlarged in 1882 with the addition of Italy to form the Triple Alliance. In 1883 Romania and Serbia became associate members. In creating the Triple Alliance, Bismarck kept France isolated and most of the European Great Powers together. In 1889 he even offered Britain associate membership of the Triple Alliance.

Even when the alliance system began to break down Bismarck was clever enough to maintain it. In 1887 Austria-Hungary refused to renew the Dreikaiserbund. Bismarck therefore signed the Reinsurance Treaty with Russia, maintaining the isolation of France.

However, the system of alliances did not always help to maintain European peace. As Source B states, Bismarck almost caused a European war with France in 1875 in the War in Sight crisis. As the Source states, this act by Bismarck seemed without clear purpose.

Also Bismarck could not prevent conflict in the Balkans. The crisis of 1875–78 led to a war between Turkey and Russia. The international crisis at the end of the war was solved by the Treaty of Berlin. In 1885–87 the Bulgarian Crisis led to the collapse of the second Dreikaiserbund.

Finally, as stated in Source C, Bismarck's alliance system was so elaborate it fell apart under his less gifted successors.

So although there was no war between European Great Powers between 1871 and 1890, Bismarck's alliances did not stop all conflict and created the potential for conflict in the future.

Q2 (a) Weltpolitik was the foreign policy of Germany after 1897. Germany planned to acquire a large overseas empire so it could become a 'world power' like Britain. In an attempt to achieve this end it built a large ocean-going navy. Weltpolitik caused considerable international tension between Germany and the other Great Powers and helped cause the First World War.

(b) Germany embarked on Weltpolitik for a variety of reasons.

Firstly, and perhaps most importantly, becoming a World Power seemed to be a natural progression in the growth of Germany. The small north German state of Prussia had become a European Great Power by the end of the 19th century. In turn, in the 1860s, Prussia had united Germany. As Europe's most powerful Great Power in terms of army and economy Germany felt it had a right to acquire a large Empire.

This desire was reinforced by the German leadership's belief that Europeans, and in particular Germans, were racially superior and had a right to occupy large parts of the world. This belief in 'Social Darwinism' made them think it was an inevitable development for mankind that Germany became a world power.

It was important to embark on Weltpolitik in 1897 because most of the world was being divided up between the European powers. In the Scramble for Africa even relatively small states such as Portugal and Belgium had acquired large amounts of territory. If Germany did not acquire territory soon it could miss out altogether.

Finally, the Kaiser's government was having problems within Germany with the rise of opposition from Socialists and Liberals. It was hoped Weltpolitik would unite the German people behind the Kaiser's government.

(c) I would agree that Weltpolitik was not very successful before 1914.

In its quest for colonies Germany acquired only a small amount of territory. It acquired the Marshall, Caroline and Samoan islands in the Pacific. It also increased its territory in Africa. These were small additions when compared to the territories acquired by Britain and France.

Weltpolitik was also not successful because it created international tension and united Germany's enemies. The first and second Moroccan crises were sparked off by German desire to acquire more territory. They had the effect of forcing Britain into agreements with its former enemies France and Russia in two Entente agreements, of 1904 and 1907. As a result, by 1909, Germany felt it was becoming surrounded by hostile, jealous powers.

Finally, the policy led Germany to build a large navy which increased conflict with Britain who saw Germany as a naval rival. The cost of building the navy put great strain on Germany's finances. This led to a rise in political opposition to the Kaiser's government from Socialists who became Germany's largest political party by 1912.

However, even though Weltpolitik did not make Germany a world power by 1914 it did have some success. Germany became one of the world's great naval powers by 1914, rivalling the Royal Navy.

Germany also acquired an empire with colonies in China, Africa and the Pacific. It also helped unite most Germans behind the government from 1897 to 1914.

Nevertheless, Germany's rulers themselves didn't regard Weltpolitik as successful by 1914 and attempted to become a world power by military means in helping to provoke the outbreak of the First World War.

AQA Unit 1 Alternative G: 'Imperial and Weimar Germany 1866–1925'

(a) The alliance of steel and rye was an important idea in Bismarck's domestic policy after 1871. 'Steel' referred to the German industrialists who had benefited from Germany's unification. Rye represented the Junker landowners of east Prussia who dominated the German state and government. Although these were the most important supporters of Bismarck there was conflict between them over economic policy. Industrialists preferred free trade. The Junkers wanted protective tariffs against cheap Russian grain. After 1879 Bismarck tended to side increasingly with the Junkers.

(b) The events of 1878–79 were very significant for German domestic affairs for a variety of reasons.

Firstly, the attempted assassination of the Kaiser by a workman allowed Bismarck to introduce the first of a series of anti-socialist laws in the Reichstag. Bismarck was fearful of the rise of the Social Democrat party. From 1878 he attempted to limit the party's growth by a mixture of repression and concessions to workers, such as the introduction of old age pensions in 1889.

The years 1878–1879 are also important because Bismarck abandoned free trade and introduced tariffs. This led to a split between Bismarck and his main supporters, the National Liberals. From 1879 Bismarck began to rely increasingly upon the support of the Conservatives. These were dominated by Junker landowners from east Prussia.

As a result of his break with the National Liberals, Bismarck also wanted to gain support from the catholic Centre Party. This led Bismarck to scale down the Kulturkampf against Catholics which had begun in 1872–73.

The overall impact of these changes meant the German Empire took a more conservative direction in internal affairs.

(c) I agree with the view that Germany's internal strengths outweighed its weaknesses in the period 1871 to 1890.

Firstly, Germany was mainland Europe's major economic power. In the period 1871 to 1890 German industry grew at a rapid rate. Industrial areas such as the Ruhr and Upper Silesia became major producers of coal and steel.

Germany's economic might helped maintain it as Europe's greatest military power. Following the defeats of Austria in 1866 and France in 1870–71, Germany remained the unrivalled military power of the continent.

Politically, Germany had a strong government under Bismarck, supported by a very efficient civil service. This made Germany the most effectively governed state on mainland Europe.

Germany was also one of a minority of states with a democratically elected national parliament. The Reichstag was elected every four years by all adult males over the age of 25. This led to the development of a party system which represented a wide cross-section of Germans from conservatives to socialists.

However, the German Empire did possess a number of weaknesses. Although the Reichstag was elected democratically, it had little political power. This was mainly in the hands of the Kaiser. As a result, the state was dominated by an unrepresentative Prussian conservative elite of Junkers.

The rapid growth of the German economy led to the increase in size of the industrial middle and working classes. These groups increasingly demanded a greater say in political affairs which created tensions within Germany.

Finally, the armed forces also possessed considerable political influence. This helped to increase the power of the Prussian landowning class and proved that Germany was not really a democratic state at all.

On balance, I think Germany's strengths outweighed its weaknesses. But these weaknesses increased in the years after 1871, creating a major political crisis in Germany by 1914.

OCR Unit 3: 'Europe 1825–1890'

(a) Prussia was able to dominate Germany after 1871 for a wide variety of reasons.

Firstly, the most important reason was that under the German Constitution of 1871, Prussia retained considerable power. The King of Prussia became the German Emperor. The Minister-President of Prussia, Bismarck became the German Chancellor.

The Constitution gave the Emperor immense power. He could hire and fire the government. He was commander of the armed forces and had the power to make international treaties and declare war.

The new German Empire was dominated by the rich landowning class of east Prussia, the Junkers. They filled most of the senior posts in the Government. They also dominated the officer class of the army. Bismarck was a Junker. After 1879, Bismarck began to rely increasingly on conservative Junker support.

After 1871 Germany was a federal state. This meant that certain political powers were exercised by individual states. These included control of education, law and order and welfare. Prussia comprised two-thirds of Germany. This made Prussia the dominant state. It also had 58 seats in the Upper House of the national parliament, the Bundesrat. This gave it the power of veto over all laws.

Finally, Prussia contained Germany's most important economic regions, the Ruhr and Upper Silesia. This made Prussia very powerful economically.

(b) In foreign policy after 1871 Bismarck aimed to isolate France and keep Europe at peace.

In many ways Bismarck was successful. He helped create a series of international agreements and alliances to keep France isolated. In 1873 he created the Dreikaiserbund which included Germany, Austria-Hungary and Russia. Even when this agreement came to an end in 1877 he was able to resurrect it, in slightly different form, in 1881.

Following the collapse of the first Dreikaiserbund Bismarck formed a secret alliance with Austria-Hungary – the Dual Alliance in 1879. This was expanded in 1882 to include Italy, becoming the Triple Alliance. In 1883 Romania and Serbia became associate members. In 1889 Bismarck even invited Britain to join. The British Prime Minister, Lord Salisbury, refused.

Even when Austria-Hungary and Russia refused to stay in alliance Bismarck was successful in keeping France isolated. After the collapse of the second Dreikaiserbund, in 1887, Bismarck signed a secret alliance with Russia – the Reinsurance Treaty.

Therefore, by 1890 Bismarck was successful in one of his main aims: keeping France isolated diplomatically. This did not mean Bismarck was always successful in his dealing with France. In

1875 in the 'War in Sight' crisis Britain and Russia forced Bismarck to back down from launching a preventive war against France.

In maintaining European peace, Bismarck was partly successful. There were no Great Power wars after 1871. Yet crisis and conflict did occur in the Balkans in 1875–78 and again in 1885–87. In both crises, a local war occurred. In 1877–78 there was the Russo–Turkish war and in 1886 the Serbo–Bulgarian War. Bismarck, on both occasions, used his diplomatic skill to limit the conflict. In 1878, in Berlin, he acted as the 'honest broker' at an international congress which brought peace back to the Balkans. In 1887 peace was maintained through the signing of the Reinsurance Treaty.

On balance, Bismarck was successful. Yet his alliance system increased suspicion and tension in European affairs. Only two years after his fall the isolation of France came to an end.

4 Russia 1855–1917

How to score full marks

AQA Unit 1 Alternative F: 'Tsarist and Revolutionary Russia 1855–1917'

(a) The Russian working people, mentioned in Source A, complained about their lives in 1905 for several reasons. Firstly, the rapid industrialisation of parts of the Russian economy in the years before 1905 had resulted in poor working conditions in factories such as the Putilov Engineering Works in St Petersburg. Also, these industrial workers faced very poor living conditions. As stated in the source, they felt 'treated as slaves' and 'impoverished'. Finally, the Russian political system was autocratic with power residing in the Tsar. This meant that working people had no political rights – a point mentioned in the concluding line of the source.

(b) The author of Source C challenges the views made in Source B in a number of ways.

Firstly, Source B suggests that important gains were made by the 1905 Revolution. In particular it refers to the rights given in the October Manifesto such as freedom of speech and conscience even though these were granted reluctantly by the Tsar.

An important reason why the sources differ is that Source B was written in the USSR in 1976. This would contain the official communist version of events. As a result, Source B suggests that the 1905 Revolution failed because of divisions between workers. Only an alliance led by the Bolshevik Party would succeed.

Source C, as a western source, does not have a political motive in writing about events. As a result, it offers a more objective view which places the events of 1905 in broader historical context and refers specifically to gains made rather than reasons for defeat.

(c) Following the 1905 Revolution the Tsarist government made important concessions.

As stated in Source C, the October Manifesto created a new parliament, the Duma, and gave fundamental freedoms to the Russian people. This helped to split the revolutionary opposition to the Tsar and helped it to survive the revolution.

Following the Revolution the Tsarist government made many important changes. Under the prime ministership of Prince Peter Stolypin, peasants were encouraged to buy land and the Duma played a role in the government of Russia. However, the Tsar retained considerable political power. In the Fundamental Law of 1906 he still had the power to hire and fire ministers.

The social and economic problems faced by working people, as mentioned in Source A, such as impoverishment and unbearable work still persisted. From 1912 to 1914, Russia was again hit by a wave of strikes which threatened the stability of the state.

Nevertheless, as suggested in Source B, workers and peasants remained divided, which helped to prevent the outbreak of another revolution.

Therefore, the Tsarist regime survived partly because it made concessions which divided the political opposition. It also survived because the mass of the population was not united in supporting an alternative to the Tsarist regime.

To ensure political opponents did not threaten the regime, the Tsar's government used repression. In the immediate aftermath of the 1905 revolution right-wing groups, known as the Black Hundreds, hunted down political opponents. Hundreds were executed. Thousands were imprisoned. Using the secret police, the Okhrana, the government dealt harshly with all opponents.

In summary, the Tsarist regime survived for a variety of reasons. The most important was its ability to make concessions and pass reforms. However, it also used repression. Yet its political opponents had little in common other than a general dislike of the regime and remained disunited.

Edexcel Unit 1: 'Russia in Revolution 1905–1917'

(a) From Source 1 it can be inferred that Russia suffered badly from poor communications. This was due both to the size of the country and the poor quality of government. The President of the Duma had to talk separately to each minister responsible suggesting a lack of government coordination.

Another factor which can be inferred is the government's fear of political change. Even though the President of the national parliament (the Duma) wanted to discuss supply problems for the army, the ministers concerned feared he really wanted to discuss political changes.

(b) The Russian economy was ill equipped to meet the demands of war for a variety of reasons.

Firstly, Russia was a vast country comprising 20% of the world's land surface. The problem of size was compounded by economic under-development. It also had very poor internal communications. The railway network was limited. Roads were dirt tracks, which became mud in spring and wet weather. Both Witte in the 1890s and Stolypin from 1907 to 1911 had attempted to modernise the economy but with very limited success. By 1914–17 Russia was still a very backward country economically. It had not developed effectively since the emancipation of serfs in 1861. Over 80% of the population were peasants farming small holdings of land.

These economic problems were made worse by poor government. Fearing political change Russia's leaders were fearful of rapid industrial change. From 1914 to 1917, Russia was led by an inefficient government which found it increasingly difficult to cope with the strains of war.

(c) Source 2 supports the message of Source 3 to a certain extent. The cartoon in Source 3 suggests that both the Tsar and Tsarina were puppets of Rasputin. They are depicted in the cartoon as Rasputin's children or playthings. This is supported in Source 2 where the Tsarina states in her letter that without Rasputin 'all would ... have been finished'. This is supported by the fact that the Tsarina was forced to write the letter to the Tsar because Grand Duke Nicholas Mikhailovich had stated that both the Tsar and Tsarina were under Rasputin's influence.

However, there is no evidence in Source 2 to suggest that the Tsar himself was under Rasputin's control. Also although the Tsarina defends Rasputin in Source 2 it does state that she was not necessarily under Rasputin's control but may have relied on him for advice.

(d) Source 3 is of value to a historian because it shows the type of cartoon that was produced in Russia in 1916. It suggests that even though Russia was at war censorship was not in place. Its anti-Tsarist message is clear. However, it is only one cartoon and may not be representative of the views of the majority of Russians at the time. Further evidence from the period would be required to corroborate the evidence. It is useful for showing the views of some Russians in late 1916 but not for 1917.

Source 4 is of value because it is a police report of January 1917. It provides an insight into how the Okhrana appraised the political and industrial situation at that time. It does state the purpose of the report. As an internal, private report it is useful in reflecting the official view of the situation. However, a public document might be unreliable as evidence because it might be trying to get over a particular viewpoint.

(e) The fall of the Tsar in February 1917 was partly due to the length of the war.

This view is supported by Source 5 when Michael Lynch states that the cumulative effect of a long war proved too destructive for the regime. This is backed up by Source 4, the Okhrana Report. By January 1917 both workers and peasants seem to be facing major economic hardship. This was leading directly to a revolutionary situation, which threatened the regime.

It is clear that the immediate conditions surrounding the fall of the Tsar were associated with the length of the war. The February Revolution was unplanned. It was caused by a combination of economic hardship and disillusionment brought on by military defeat. The strains of war had led to rising prices and food shortages. These were the main causes of the demonstrations in Petrograd in February 1917.

The Tsar fell also because of disillusionment with his military and political leadership. He was opposed by many conservatives as well as radicals because of this. The Tsar was forced to abdicate because many wanted Tsarism to survive rather than fall.

Yet for all the problems associated with the war Tsardom fell because of long-term problems. Tsar Nicholas II was an inept ruler who was very reluctant to give up political power. This helped create the revolutionary situation in 1905 as well as 1917. The Russian state was economically and socially backward. This built up major tensions within society, which came to the fore during the war.

Faced with long-term political and social problems, the war merely brought these to a head. The strains of a long war were too great for a weakly led and backward government to survive.

OCR Unit 3: 'Europe 1890–1945 (Russia 1894–1917)'

(a) In the period 1906 to 1914 the Russian government made many political and social reforms.

Following the 1905 Revolution the most important political reform was the October Manifesto which became law in the Fundamental Law of 1906. This ended the autocracy in Russia where the Tsar had sole political power. It created an elected national parliament, the Duma, for the first time. It also allowed freedom of speech and religion.

However, political change was limited. The Tsar still had the power to hire and fire ministers. Under Prime Minister Stolypin, from 1907 to 1911, the right to vote for the Duma was restricted. The Duma from 1907 onwards was more conservative and had little political power.

The Tsar's power was also maintained through political repression. The secret police, the Okhrana, rounded up and imprisoned political opponents in large numbers. Many were sent to internal exile in Siberia.

In social affairs Prince Peter Stolypin attempted to win support for the Tsarist regime by aiding the peasants. Between 1907 and 1911 he made it easier for peasants to leave the commune. He created a land bank where they could acquire cheap loans to buy their own land. As independent landowners it was hoped they would support the Tsar.

Unfortunately, little or nothing was done to help industrial workers. They still faced very poor living and working conditions. This resulted in a wave of strikes from 1912 to 1914. The government reacted with repression, as was shown in the Lena Goldfields massacre of 1912.

Overall, the government did make some important changes but Russia remained an economically backward state with political repression.

(b) Russia's involvement in the First World War was a major reason in bringing about the February Revolution of 1917.

The war placed major strains on what was a backward, undeveloped country. The railway network was limited. Roads were dirt tracks, impassable in the spring and wet weather. Although it contained some industrial areas, most of the population were engaged in subsistence agriculture. This resulted in a rise in prices and food shortages as the war progressed. The February Revolution was unplanned. It began as demonstrations in Petrograd about food shortages.

These demonstrations quickly became political because of the general disillusionment with the Tsar's handling of the war. He was held directly responsible because he was commander of the army from April 1915. From that date the Russian army faced defeat at the hands of the German and Austro-Hungarian armies. By February 1917 Poland and most of White Russia had been occupied by the enemy. Mutinies began to take place in the army over the winter of 1916–17.

His government was discredited because of the widespread belief that Rasputin was in control of both the Tsar and Tsarina. Even though Rasputin was assassinated in late 1916, the government remained weak and inefficient.

Yet to see the fall of the Tsar as a result of the war would be an exaggeration. Even by 1914 the Russian state was facing major problems. It was economically backward. Over 80% were peasants. They faced poor living and working conditions. These problems created major tensions within Russian society.

Politically, Russia was seen as backward compared to other European states. There was a major demand for more political reform, which the Tsar was reluctant to make. Revolutionary groups such as Social Revolutionaries, Mensheviks and Bolsheviks were plotting to bring down the state.

Therefore, the war brought to a head serious political and social problems which already existed by 1914.

5 International relations 1890–1939

How to score full marks

OCR Unit 3 'Europe 1890–1945: The Causes and Impact of the First World War: 1890–1920'

(a) The First World War had a major impact on all those who took part. It had a profound impact on Germany.

The War led to a political revolution, which had a major impact on the civilian population. The fear of impending military defeat forced the German High Command to hand power to a civilian government in October 1918. This event sparked off a political revolution. Mutinies of soldiers and sailors helped to undermine the Kaiser's regime. By early November 1918 the Kaiser was forced to abdicate and flee to Holland. In his place a democratic republic was declared. For the first time in German history the government was dependent on majority support in the Reichstag. Philip Scheidemann, a Social Democrat, became Germany's first democratic head of government.

These political changes were in part brought about by the economic impact of the war on the German civilian population. The Allied economic blockade and the economic strains of war had created major problems. Food shortages led to the development of ersatz or substitute foods such as nettle tea. The winter of 1915–16 was known as the Turnip Winter as German civilians had to rely on root crops to survive. By the summer of 1916 food riots were commonplace in many cities. Such hardship increased hostility towards the Kaiser's regime and helped bring the political revolution of late 1918.

(b) The stalemate of the First World War came to an end in 1918 for several reasons.

The most important was the failure of the German Spring Offensive on the Western Front. Even though the Germans made an initial breakthrough they were stopped at the Second Battle of the Marne. This was due to a number of reasons. Firstly, the Germans had suffered heavy casualties in their offensive. They no longer had the supplies of manpower to replenish the losses. Also, it was due to effective leadership by the new Allied supreme commander Marshall Foch. In addition, the Allies had the advantage in men and material.

The Western Allies benefited enormously from the entry of the USA into the war from 1917. In war supplies and extra men the Americans helped tip the balance in favour of the Allies.

In contrast, as the war went on the Allied Blockade helped starve Germany into submission. By late 1918 Germany was facing food riots and mutinies among both soldiers and sailors. The blockade had created a revolutionary situation inside Germany.

Germany was not the only Central Power to face difficulty. By October 1918 Austria-Hungary was facing defeat by Italy and the Western Allies from Salonika in Greece would have attacked Serbia. By October 1918 Austria-Hungary, Bulgaria and Turkey sued for peace with the Allies. These developments undermined the German war effort helping end the stalemate.

Therefore, the stalemate was broken primarily because Germany and its Allies could no longer match the Western Allies in men and material to sustain the war effort.

AQA Unit 1 Alternative H: 'The Emergence of the Super Powers and the New World Order 1900–1962'

(a) According to Source A, the most important economic factor in the decline of the major European powers was the debts they owed to the USA as a result of the War. In the War the western Allies, Britain and France, had purchased large amounts of armaments on credit. However, there were other economic reasons. France and Germany had suffered severe economic strains in fighting the war. Parts of northern France were devastated. In Russia the Tsar had been overthrown and the country entered a period of economic and political turmoil.

(b) The author of Source C challenges the views of Source B in a number of ways. Source C claims the Versailles settlement was a success. The author calls it a 'creditable achievement'. This stands in contrast to the views in Source B which regard it as 'a conspicuous failure'.

Both authors accept that the settlement collapsed in the inter-war period with the rise of Nazi Germany. However, Source C suggests this was not due to the settlement but the failure of the inter-war political leaders, in particular those in Britain and France, to enforce the settlement. The writer is accusing those who appeased Hitler in the 1930s. The author of Source B, in contrast, regards the treaty as fatally flawed and was the cause of the rise of Hitler.

Therefore, Source C challenges Source B on the issue of who was to blame for the collapse of the Versailles settlement in the inter-war period.

(c) The First World War and the treaties that followed it were important in eroding Europe's primacy in the world.

The War caused enormous damage to the European economy. Millions died; even more were wounded. The major combatants – Britain, France, Germany and Russia – all virtually bankrupted themselves in fighting such a long and destructive war. As Source A suggests, after 1918 the major European countries became debtors to the USA. The war also led to the collapse of four European Empires – Germany, Austria-Hungary, Russia and Turkey. In Russia the Tsar was overthrown and the state faced a destructive revolutionary period followed by civil war.

The peace treaties also help to explain Europe's decline. Source B suggests that the Versailles settlement created serious problems for inter-war Europe. The reparations and war guilt issues created tremendous resentment in Germany and greatly assisted the rise of Hitler. However, the author of Source C disagrees, claiming it was politicians in the 1930s who were mainly to blame for inter-war problems.

The War also assisted European decline, as stated in Source A, because it encouraged nationalist revolts against European colonial rule. This was most apparent in British India and Ireland. However, it also affected the French Empire.

There were other reasons for European decline. From the beginning of the 20th century the USA was fast becoming the world's major economic power. The War accelerated the process. But in the 1920s the USA experienced a major economic boom which confirmed its status as the world's greatest economy.

Similarly, Japan had industrialised by 1900. The Japanese began to dominate large parts of East Asia economically. Also in 1910 it had acquired Korea and became a major influence in East China by 1919. Japan was also able to acquire economic markets vacated by Britain because of the war.

Therefore, the war and the peace treaties were the most important reasons for the erosion of Europe's primacy in the world. However, there were also long-term factors, such as the rise of the USA and Japan which had preceded the war.

OCR Unit 3: 'Europe and the World 1919–1989'

'International Relations 1919–1939'

(a) Although united in their desire to defeat Germany the peacemakers after the First World War all had different aims.

The French, under Prime Minister Clemenceau, wanted to cripple Germany militarily. On two occasions – 1870 and 1914 – France had been invaded by Germany. Clemenceau wanted to prevent such an occurrence happening again. In addition to destroying Germany's ability to fight another aggressive war, he also wanted Germany to pay for the damage inflicted on France. For over four years large parts of northern France had been devastated by war. France had also suffered millions of casualties. They expected Germany to pay for these. As a result, the French demanded large reparations and a demilitarised Rhineland.

Britain had similar views. They wanted to destroy German naval power which had been a threat to Britain. They also wanted Germany to pay reparations. Lloyd George, the Prime Minister, wanted to build 'homes fit for heroes'. The Germans were expected to pay for these. However, unlike the French, the British did not want to deal too severely with Germany. Lloyd George feared that communism would spread to Germany if the Germans were forced to accept too harsh a peace treaty.

The Americans, on the other hand, did not wish to force Germany to pay reparations. However, President Wilson did want to prevent future war. He was in favour of redrawing the political map of Europe based on national self-determination. This would involve the creation of states based on national groups. He believed the First World War had been caused primarily because of nationalism. Wilson also wanted to create a League of Nations where all the world's countries would join to help preserve peace.

(b) The outbreak of the Second World War in Europe has usually been attributed to Germany alone.

In many ways Germany must bear the main responsibility. Once he became German leader Hitler aimed to destroy the Versailles settlement. In doing so he quickly rearmed Germany. More importantly, he aimed to unite all Germans into one state. This led to the Anschluss of March 1939 and the Sudetenland crisis of September 1938. However, the main responsibility was Hitler's desire to create 'living space' (lebensraum) for the German people in eastern Europe. This would also involve destroying the USSR as the centre of world communism. As part of this aim Hitler invaded Poland in September 1939, which sparked off the war.

However, Germany was not solely responsible. Both Britain and France must accept a share of responsibility. Neither power was willing to support the Versailles settlement in the 1930s. This was shown by both countries' inactivity in 1936 when Hitler broke the Versailles and Locarno treaties by remilitarising the Rhineland.

More significantly, it was the British and French policy of appeasement of Hitler over Austria and the Sudetenland which encouraged Hitler to believe he could achieve his aims in eastern Europe. In the case of the latter, instead of defending Czechoslovakia, Britain and France helped Hitler destroy the state. In the Munich Agreement of September 1938 they gave the Sudetenland to Germany, against the wishes of the Czech government. This led directly to the partition of the Czech state with both Poland and Hungary acquiring former Czechoslovak territory. The agreement also encouraged Hitler to acquire more territory in central and east Europe. In March 1939 he took over what was left of the Czech lands. Slovakia became a separate state under German protection.

Only after the German occupation of Bohemia-Moravia, in March 1939, did Britain and France abandon appeasement. They then both guaranteed Polish independence. When Hitler invaded Poland in September 1939 the British and French were faced with little alternative but to declare war on Germany.

Therefore, Germany must bear the main responsibility for the outbreak of the Second World War in 1939. However, neither Britain nor France was willing to defend the Versailles settlement during the 1903s until it was too late to prevent war.

6 Russia/Soviet Union 1917–1929

How to score full marks

Edexcel Unit 2: 'The Triumph of Bolshevism? Russia 1918–1929'

 (a) In many ways the seizure of power by the Bolsheviks, in November 1917, was a relatively easy task. It was far more difficult to keep control after that event.

The most immediate way of keeping control was to end Russia's participation in the First World War. They had campaigned on the slogan of 'Peace, Bread, Land'. By December the Bolsheviks had negotiated a ceasefire with the Germans on the Eastern Front. More difficult was negotiating a peace treaty. Lenin was forced to accept a very harsh treaty, the Treaty of Brest-Litovsk, in order to end the war. Almost 25% of Russian territory was lost, which included valuable agricultural land.

The peace treaty itself created problems. It forced the Left Social Revolutionaries to leave the coalition government with the Bolsheviks. The treaty was also deeply unpopular within the Bolshevik Party and almost led to a split.

The Bolsheviks also had to face the problem created by the election to the Constituent Assembly that took place in December 1917. They received only 25% of the vote and seats. The Social Revolutionaries were the largest party. To keep control, the Bolshevik government dissolved the Assembly after only one day in January 1918. This made civil war more likely.

Both of these events helped spark off an attempted revolution by Left Social Revolutionaries in the summer of 1918. Even Lenin faced an assassination attempt. To survive, the Bolsheviks resorted to the use of repression and terror. The secret police (Cheka) arrested and imprisoned thousands of political opponents.

The attempted revolution was part of the Civil War where the Bolsheviks faced their political opponents. This was the most important problem they faced. Between 1918 and 1921, the Bolsheviks successfully defeated White armies in a vicious civil war. To make matters worse the White armies were supported by foreign troops from Britain, France, the USA, Italy and Japan. To keep control, the Bolsheviks founded the Red

Army under the leadership of Trotsky. The Red Army was able to use its control of the Russian heartland between Petrograd and Moscow to defeat each White army in turn.

Even though they had won the civil war by 1921, the Bolsheviks still faced problems. They had introduced state control of the economy during the civil war. This was called War Communism. It led to a major drop in production and helped to create famine in the countryside. It also sparked off a rebellion against Bolshevik rule by sailors of the Baltic fleet – the Kronstadt Rebellion of March 1921. As a result, Lenin replaced War Communism with the New Economic Policy (NEP) in the same month. This allowed private enterprise in small businesses and farms.

Therefore, by the time of Lenin's death the Bolsheviks had used a variety of methods to keep control. The most important was the use of repression and terror. However, leaving the First World War and changing economic policy were also important.

(b) When Lenin died in 1924 he had no obvious successor. Yet by 1929 Stalin had become the undisputed leader of the USSR.

The most important reason why Stalin succeeded Lenin was the fact that he had acquired considerable power within the Communist Party. In 1917 he became a member of the Politburo as Commissar for Nationalities. This gave him responsibility for over half the population of Soviet Russia. In 1919 he gained control of Rabkrin. This organisation checked on the loyalty of communist party members. It enabled Stalin to appoint colleagues and supporters in the party. In the same year he became the official link between the Politburo and the civil service of the Communist Party, the Orgburo. Finally, in 1922 he was made General Secretary of the Communist Party. So by the time of Lenin's death, Stalin had already amassed enormous power within the party.

Stalin's main rival for power was Trotsky. However, he was feared by many other leading communists. To stop Trotsky becoming leader, Zinoviev and Kamenev joined forces with Stalin in 1924–25 to remove Trotsky from a position of power.

Stalin was aided in this plan by the debate about policy. Trotsky supported Permanent World Revolution and rapid industrialisation; Stalin supported Socialism in One Country. This latter policy had widespread support in the Communist Party and the country which had faced war, revolution and civil war.

Once Trotsky was defeated, Stalin was able to remove Zinoviev and Kamenev by supporting the continuation of the New Economic Policy. This allowed private enterprise for small firms and for farming. Kamenev and Zinoviev wanted rapid industrialisation. To support his view, Stalin relied on support from Tomsky in the trade union movement and Bukharin, the editor of 'Pravda' daily newspaper.

Yet in 1928, Stalin changed his view on economic policy in order to remove Bukharin and Tomsky from the government. He accepted the idea of paid industrialisation and the forced collectivisation of Soviet agriculture. He was able to win support for this change of policy because Stalin as General Secretary effectively controlled appointments to senior positions within the Communist Party.

Therefore, by 1929, Stalin was the sole leader of the USSR. He had removed opposition by cleverly changing policies to suit his needs. He was able to win support from the Communist Party because he controlled the Party machine.

Q2 (a) The Bolsheviks took a variety of steps to deal with Russia's economic problems.

In 1921, Russia was a backward state economically. Over 80% of the population were peasants, many engaged in subsistence agriculture. For a political party that wanted to create a communist society based on industry this was a major problem.

The Bolsheviks attempted to solve these problems through the introduction of War Communism. Under this policy industries were taken into public ownership. They were forced to provide material to help the Bolsheviks win the civil war. In the countryside the Bolsheviks sent out requisition squads to forcibly take grain from the peasants to help feed the towns and cities.

The economic problems were also made worse by the famine that affected much of European Russia from 1921 to 1922. This had been caused by years of political and economic instability resulting from war, revolution and civil war.

To overcome these problems the Bolsheviks introduced the New Economic Policy in 1921. This allowed small firms to be run privately. The Government kept control of 'the commanding heights of industry'. The peasants were allowed to keep their grain as long as they gave some to the government. Any surplus could be sold in markets.

The New Economic Policy lasted until 1928. In that year it was abandoned. It was replaced by the forced collectivisation of Soviet agriculture. Private farms would be replaced by large 'collective farms' (Kolkhoz) run on industrial lines. Industry was to be planned and taken over completely by the government. Targets for industrial production were set in Five Year Plans.

(b) The Communists changed their economic policies so much between 1921 and 1929 for a variety of reasons.

Firstly, they faced opposition to War Communism. In March 1921 the Baltic Fleet rebelled at Kronstadt over economic and political policy. These had been some of the most loyal supporters of the Communists.

Also, industrial and grain production had dropped considerably during the period of War Communism. Unless it was changed the country faced economic collapse. Production had fallen far below the level of before the First World War.

Even though the New Economic Policy, which replaced War Communism, proved successful in preventing economic collapse it created other problems. It encouraged private enterprise, which was against communist principles. Private traders (NEPmen) grew wealthy under the policy.

Economic policy also changed for political reasons. In Stalin's rise to power he used the debate on economic policy to defeat his opponents. Firstly, he defeated Trotsky in 1925 by supporting Socialism in One Country. In 1928, he defeated Bukharin and Tomsky by abandoning the NEP.

By 1928 industrial prices had fallen at a time when grain prices rose. This could have led to another major economic crisis. In that year the economic policy changed again to one of forced collectivisation of agriculture and planned industrialisation under government control. This was done to increase Russian economic performance greatly. Communist leaders feared anti-communist, western countries might attack them.

Finally, the policy adopted in 1928 was inevitable if the communists planned to create a socialist society in the USSR. Socialism could only be achieved if the Soviet Union became an industrialised state with a large working class. Therefore, the main reasons for changing economic policy was to ensure the survival of the Communist government allowing it the chance to build a strong, industrialised socialist society.

AQA Alternative F: 'Russia and the USSR 1855–1991'

Option B: Stalin's Rise to Power 1922–1929

When Lenin died in January 1924 there was no obvious successor. However, by 1929, Stalin had emerged as the undisputed leader of the USSR.

Although a relatively obscure Communist leader by 1924 Stalin had, nevertheless, amassed considerable political power. As a Georgian he was chosen by Lenin to be Commissar for Nationalities in the first communist government in November 1917. This position gave Stalin immediate control over half the Soviet population who were non-Russian. From November 1917, Stalin was able to appoint his supporters to the non-Russian-speaking parts of Soviet Russia. This laid the foundations for his immense bureaucratic power base.

By 1919 the Communist Party had grown rapidly. In order to check the loyalty of the new party members, Lenin set up the Commisariat of Workers and Peasants Inspectorate – known as Rabkrin. It had the power to remove anyone whose loyalty was in question. Stalin was made Commissar. This enabled him to remove from the lower levels of the Party anyone who he felt was disloyal to him. This point is made clear by Martin McCauley in his book 'Stalin and Stalinism'.

To cement the links between the political decision makers within the party and the party organisation Stalin was made liaison official between the Politburo and the Orgburo. Finally, in 1922 Lenin appointed Stalin as Party Secretary. So even before Lenin had died he had created a very strong power base.

This development had not gone unnoticed by Lenin and Trotsky. Shortly before Lenin's death, they both came to the conclusion that Stalin should be removed as General Secretary. Unfortunately, Lenin's sudden death brought this plan to an end. At a crucial moment Stalin's rise was assisted by good fortune. As mentioned by Robert Conquest in his TV documentary on Stalin, one of Lenin's private secretaries gave Stalin a copy of Lenin's Last Will and Testament where Lenin denounced Stalin. Stalin was able to limit the public announcement of Lenin's Will to a small number of Stalin supporters on the Central Committee of the Communist Party.

Nevertheless, Stalin exploited Lenin's death to his own advantage. He helped to create the 'cult' of Lenin and insisted that Lenin be laid to rest in a public mausoleum in Red Square, Moscow. From 1924 Stalin portrayed himself as a person who merely wanted to complete the work begun by Lenin. Unfortunately, Trotsky was absent from Lenin's funeral. With Stalin present it was becoming clear that he seemed to be Lenin's natural successor.

Stalin was able to become leader rather than Trotsky because Trotsky was feared by other leading communists. Stalin had founded the Red Army and was the most widely known communist leader after Lenin. He had a strong personality, was an effective public speaker and was highly intelligent. He had also joined the Bolshevik Party late in 1917. Before that date he had been a major critic of the Bolsheviks. Many communists feared he would become a Russian Napoleon destroying the Communist Revolution if he became leader.

Kamenev (Lenin's deputy) and Zinoviev (head of Comintern) conspired with Stalin to prevent Trotsky becoming leader. As three of the most important members of the Politburo, they had the collective power to defeat Trotsky.

However, Trotsky aided his own defeat by supporting the policy of Permanent World Revolution. This would have involved Soviet Russia invading the rest of Europe in order to spread communism. It was unpopular in the party for a variety of reasons. Russia was exhausted after a decade of war, revolution and civil war. An attempt to spread communism westward had failed in Soviet defeat in the Russo–Polish war of 1920–21. Finally, all attempts at communist uprisings in central Europe had failed.

Stalin, by contrast, supported Socialism in One Country. The aim was to build socialism in the USSR first before attempting to spread it abroad.

To ensure that his policy would be supported, Stalin filled the Central Committee of the Communist Party with his own supporters. Therefore, Trotsky's policy was rejected. He was removed from the Politburo, then forced into exile by 1927 in Soviet Central Asia.

Once Stalin had removed Trotsky, he still had the problem of working with Kamenev and Zinoviev. He was able to remove them from power in 1927 by opposing their call for the rapid industrialisation of Russia. Stalin supported Bukharin, the editor of 'Pravda', in defending the New Economic Policy. Using his control over the party Stalin had his two former allies expelled from the Politburo.

Within 18 months Stalin turned on his new allies, the so-called Right Opposition of Bukharin and his followers. As mentioned by Michael Lynch in 'USSR from Stalin to Khrushchev', in 1928 Stalin changed his

view and supported the forced collectivisation of Soviet agriculture and planned industrial growth. He used as a reason the fear that the USSR faced the threat of invasion from western, anti-Communist countries. Supported by the Central Committee of the Communist Party, Stalin outvoted his opponents.

By 1929 Stalin had filled the Politburo and other leading positions within the Communist Party and government with his supporters. Through a mixture of amassing bureaucratic power within the Party and clever tactics, Stalin had become the successor to Lenin.

In conclusion, Stalin rather than Trotsky became leader of the USSR because he controlled the Communist Party machine. Stalin had immense power over appointments and promotions. He was also aided by the general fear of Trotsky by several other leading communists. It was slightly ironic that in order to prevent Trotsky from becoming a dictator, other leading communists offered their support to Stalin.

AQA Alternative J: 'The Effects of World War I: 1915–1924'

Option A: The Accession to Power of the Bolsheviks and Lenin's Regime

According to the historian E. H. Carr, in 'The Bolshevik Revolution', he regarded Lenin's greatest triumph as the consolidation of power after 1917, then the taking of power in the October Revolution.

In October 1917 Lenin inherited a nation in chaos. The country had faced two revolutions within a year. The army was facing mutiny and military defeat. The people faced rapidly rising prices and food shortages. Law and order had all but collapsed.

By the time of his death, Lenin had brought a large degree of political stability to Russia. The first move in this direction was to remove Russia from the First World War. In December 1917 a ceasefire was organised for the Eastern Front. Lenin realised that unless a peace treaty could be signed with Germany and Austria-Hungary he would face political defeat. In March 1918 Lenin forced his government to accept the Treaty of Brest-Litovsk. The harsh nature of the treaty caused political instability. The Left Social Revolutionaries left the coalition government with the Bolsheviks. Even worse, the Bolshevik Party almost split over the issue.

What made matters worse for Lenin in the period after gaining power was the result of the Constituent Assembly elections of December 1917. The Bolsheviks gained only 25% of the vote. The largest party was the Social Revolutionaries who supported the peasants. In January 1918 Lenin was faced with the possibility of a Constituent Assembly producing an anti-Bolshevik, democratic constitution. He therefore closed down the Assembly after only one day.

These events helped spark off a civil war and attempted revolution against the Bolsheviks. In the summer of 1918 the Left Social Revolutionaries launched a revolution. Even Lenin faced and survived an assassination attempt. To ensure political control Lenin resorted to the use of terror and repression. The communist secret police, the Cheka, were used to arrest and imprison thousands of political opponents. Labour camps were created to house these prisoners. Under Lenin's regime the Gulag system of concentration camps became a permanent feature of Communist rule.

The main threat to political stability in this period was the Civil War. Under Lenin's political leadership and Trotsky's military leadership, the Bolsheviks were able to defeat their anti-communist opponents. From a political base centred on Petrograd and Moscow, the Bolsheviks extended their political control to all European Russia by the summer of 1921.

To increase political stability and control at the end of the civil war Lenin made important changes at the 10th Party Congress of March 1921. He banned all political parties other than the communists. He also banned factions within the Communist Party. By introducing the idea of 'democratic centralism', Lenin made sure that he was the effective ruler of the state.

However, even though the Bolsheviks won the civil war they still had to rule a multi-racial state where Russians were actually in a slight minority. In 1922 Lenin created the USSR. This gave the impression that the Communist state was made up of a collection of different national republics. However, the Communist Party was in effective control of each of the Soviet Republics.

By the time of Lenin's death, the Bolsheviks had brought political stability to most of the USSR. However, they still did not effectively control Central Asia. This region remained outside effective control until the late 1920s.

While Lenin's regime brought a large degree of political stability, it had less success in bringing economic stability. In 1917 Russia was still a backward country with over 80% of the population working as peasants. It had suffered badly from the strains of a world war. In order to win the civil war and to introduce socialism, Lenin created War Communism. It meant all factories came under state control. Grain was forcibly taken from the peasants to feed the people in towns and cities. Although popular with party members, War Communism led to a major drop in industrial and food production. This resulted in famine in 1920 to 1921.

In order to bring economic stability to Russia Lenin introduced the New Economic Policy in March 1921. This allowed private enterprise in small business. The main industries, such as coal and steel, remained in government hands. Peasants were also allowed to keep their grain once they had given a proportion to the government. This development allowed the reopening of private markets where goods and food could be bought and sold privately.

By the time of Lenin's death, economic collapse had been averted. However, it did lead to the growth of a class of rich, private traders known as NEPmen who benefited directly from the reintroduction of some form of private enterprise.

In a social sense the USSR was still potentially unstable by the time of Lenin's death. The country was ruled by a party that was committed to the introduction of socialism. This involved the creation of a large working class and state ownership of the economy. Instead the USSR was a land of peasants who worked on privately owned small farms. Lenin referred to the USSR as a union of workers and peasants. If the USSR was to become a truly socialist state a social as well as a political revolution would have to take place. It was Stalin's task to bring about the social and economic revolution which was to make the USSR a communist state by 1941.

How to score full marks

Edexcel Unit 3: 'Life in the Soviet Union 1928–1941'

(a) In Source 1 Stalin emphasises the need to create socialism. In doing so the Soviet Union needs to industrialise. He states that the country should modernise. This would lead to a socialist Russia overtaking capitalist countries in economic development. This would show that socialism was superior to capitalism as an economic system.

However, in Source 2 Stalin offers a different emphasis for industrialisation. It is because the USSR is threatened with possible attack from advanced (capitalist) countries. The USSR has to learn from the past when its economic backwardness led to military defeat, as in the First World War.

(b) When the USSR embarked on planned rapid industrialisation it was important to have an effective food supply to the cities. Under War Communism, between 1918 and 1921, and the NEP, between 1921 and 1929, it was felt that the peasant might hold back grain. As a complement to industrialisation, Soviet agriculture was put on a business footing. Small peasant holdings were merged into large farms, which had the benefit of modern farm machinery. When collectivisation occurred it destroyed the kulak class. Many of those who opposed collectivisation were forced to work in the achievement of the Five Year Plan, thereby aiding industrialisation.

However, in reality, forced collectivisation also harmed industrialisation. The policy led to the destruction of much of Russia's livestock. Collective farms were not efficiently run and the hoped for increase in food supply did not materialise.

(c) In many ways the lives of the mass of the Russian people did improve as a result of Stalin's economic policies between 1929 and 1941.

The Five Year Plans helped create a modern industrial state. Tens of thousands flocked to cities to find work. The industrialisation programme provided job opportunities for engineers, planners and managers, as well as ordinary workers.

In addition to providing work the economic policies provided additional advantages. The Moscow metro was built giving the capital a modern transport system. The Dneipr Dam provided hydro-electric power and electricity.

By 1941 more Russians lived in urban areas than in the countryside. They were able to benefit from a vastly improved educational system which led to most Russians being literate and numerate by 1941.

However, not all economic policies benefited the mass of the Russian people. Forced collectivisation created misery for many peasants. Thousands were killed for opposing the policy. Tens of thousands were forced into collective farms against their will. Between 1932 and 1933 millions died in a man-made famine in the Ukraine caused by the collectivisation and industrialisation policies. The policy also resulted in a drop in farm production, in particular in meat.

The policies also harmed most Russians because many were forced at random to work in slave labour camps. The Belamor Canal, linking the Baltic and White seas, was constructed by forced labour – most of them innocent victims of Stalin's secret police.

OCR Unit 3: 'Europe and the World 1919–1939'

The USSR 1924–1953

(a) Stalin became leader of the Soviet Union for several reasons.

The most important reason was Stalin's ability to amass considerable power within the Communist Party and government by 1924. In 1917 he was made Commissar for Nationalities. This gave him direct control of around half the Soviet population who were non-Russian. In 1919 he acquired control of Rabkrin, a department which checked on the loyalty of Communist Party members. These posts allowed Stalin to build up a power base through the appointment of supporters.

In 1922 he was appointed General Secretary of the Party. So even before Lenin's death Stalin was running the Communist Party from his position of Secretary.

Once Lenin died, Stalin benefited from the suspicion and fear felt by many leading Communists against Trotsky. Trotsky had seemed to be the likely successor to Lenin. He had founded the Red Army and won the civil war. To stop Trotsky becoming leader, Zinoviev and Kamenev sided with Stalin.

They were able to defeat Trotsky partly because of Stalin's control over much of the membership of the Central Committee of the Communist Party. They also benefited because Stalin supported the policy of Socialism in One

Country. This was more popular with party members than Trotsky's policy of Permanent World Revolution. That policy would have involved war with other European states.

Stalin was able to remove from government first Kamenev and Zinoviev and then Bukharin and Rykov because of his support for different economic policies between 1926 and 1929. In 1926–27 he supported continuing the New Economic Policy, against Zinoviev's and Kamenev's plan for industrialisation. In 1928 Stalin reversed his views and supported industrialisation, which led to the removal from government of Bukharin and Rykov.

Therefore, by 1929 Stalin became sole leader of the USSR. It was mainly due to his control of the Communist Party but was also aided by his ability to change policy when it suited him.

(b) Stalin brought about many changes in the USSR in the 1930s.

The most important changes occurred in economic policy. The introduction of forced collectivisation of Soviet agriculture destroyed the independent peasant class. These comprised 80% of Russia's population. In doing so Stalin removed a rival to communist control. However, it also involved the destruction of much livestock and a man-made famine in the Ukraine in 1932–33 was a direct result of this policy.

Stalin also made profound changes to Soviet industry. The first three Five Year Plans transformed the USSR into a major industrial power by the end of the decade. Completely new industrial cities were created, such as Magnitogorsk. Also, by 1941 more Russians lived in urban areas than the countryside.

In political matters Stalin created an absolute dictatorship where no one was expected to question his authority. This was established through the Purges of 1934 to 1939. Millions were arrested, imprisoned or executed. These included all the leading members of the Communist Party such as Kamenev, Zinoviev and Bukharin. Stalin also destroyed the officer class of the Soviet armed forces because he feared they might challenge his authority.

However, in other respects, there was little change. Stalin had already established himself as dictator of the USSR by 1929. In the 1930s, he merely consolidated his control on power.

Also the rule of the Communist Party remained unchallenged. The USSR remained firmly under the control of the Party throughout the decade.

Even though terror was used on a large scale during the Purges, the system had already been established during Lenin's regime. The system of Gulag concentration camps already existed across the USSR by 1930. Also, the secret terror police had been created by Lenin. Known initially as the Cheka, it had become the NKVD after 1934.

Therefore, Stalin did bring considerable change to the USSR during the 1930s. There was a complete change in economic policy. However, the political dictatorship which was already in existence in 1930 was made more severe.

AQA Unit 1 Alternative J: 'The Origins and Consolidation of Totalitarian Regimes 1918–1939'

(a) The term 'counter revolution', as used in the USSR in the 1930s, came to mean anyone who stood in the way of Stalin. Initially, managers and planners of the first Five Year Plan were accused of working with foreign powers when targets were not achieved. It also referred to those who opposed forced collectivisation. Even though they may not have been rich, many peasants were accused of having a 'kulak mentality'. Eventually, the tens of thousands arrested during the Purges were branded counter-revolutionary even though most were innocent of any charge.

(b) Stalin accused many of 'treachery and counter-revolution' in the 1930s for a variety of reasons.

Firstly, he used the terms as part of his programme to remove potential political rivals within the Communist Party. Even former leaders were accused. Usually they were accused of plotting with Trotsky or capitalist countries to undermine the USSR. This was done during the Great Purges from 1934. Leaders such as Zinoviev who led Comintern and Lenin's former deputy, Kamenev, were accused in this way.

The term was also used against individuals for supposedly sabotaging the Five Year Plans. Instead of accepting that errors in planning or material shortages were to blame, Stalin and the secret police accused individuals at random using these phrases.

Finally, the term was used against those who opposed forced collectivisation. Anyone who was unwilling to see the benefits of the change was accused of undermining the USSR and socialism.

Therefore, Stalin used these terms to accuse anyone of acting against his wishes or using them as scapegoats for any shortcomings of his economic or political policies.

(c) To a large extent Stalin did remove 'treachery and counter-revolution' as he saw it during the 1930s.

The Great Purges of 1934–39 saw the removal of all the potential political rivals to Stalin for leadership of the USSR. The Purges began with the assassination of Sergei Kirov on Stalin's express orders. By 1939 all potential leaders, including all those who had served in Lenin's Politburo, had been executed.

In addition, Stalin removed all the leading members of the Soviet armed forces. In the Army Show Trail of 1937 Marshall Tukachevsky and the other senior generals were tried and executed.

Ordinary Soviet citizens were not immune from this process. The secret police arrested people at random and imprisoned them for crimes against the USSR. This so-called period of High Stalinism (1934–39) used terror for terror's sake. It created an atmosphere where no one was willing to criticise Stalin or his policies.

However, many of Stalin's attempts to remove 'treachery and counter-revolution' were not successful. In particular, the forced collectivisation of Soviet agriculture had a devastating effect. Livestock numbers dropped drastically as peasants slaughtered them instead of allowing them to be used in collective farms. Also, Stalin's policy led to a famine in the Ukraine between 1932 and 1933. This resulted in the loss of millions of lives. All of these developments resulted in a major drop in farm production.

Also, Stalin's claim that he was removing treachery from the forces had an adverse effect on the performance of the armed forces. In 1940 the Red Army struggled to defeat Finland in the Winter War. In 1941 the army suffered massive defeats by the Germans at the beginning of Operation Barbarossa.

The attempt to root out traitors and counter-revolutionaries from industry had the effect of removing good managers and administrators. It also prevented managers complaining to the authorities for fear of imprisonment, or worse, at the hands of the secret police.

8 Italy 1918–1939

How to score full marks

Edexcel Unit 2: 'Italy: The Rise of Fascism 1918–1925'

Q1 (a) The Fascist Party was created after the First World War. It grew out of Italian disillusionment with the peace treaties that ended the war. Italy had been promised territory by the Allies, which it did not receive. In addition, Fascists accused the liberal politicians of offering weak leadership for Italy, which resulted in unstable government. The Fascist Party was nationalist, anti-democratic and anti-socialist.

Although it was founded in 1919 fascism did not gain popularity until it became overtly anti-socialist and anti-communist during the Red Year of 1919. The Fascist Party began to attract supporters who feared left-wing political ideas. These supporters had also lost faith in the liberal politicians of Italy in offering an effective opposition to the Left.

By 1921 Italy faced political instability as government followed government. In that year, Italy had three prime ministers. This instability was matched by the continued growth of socialist and communist groups. The only party that seemed to stand up to the Left was the Fascist Party. Squadristi bands (squads of uniformed Fascists) attacked socialist newspapers and trade union buildings. By the end of 1921 the Fascists seemed to be the only party to stand between socialism and a takeover of power.

In its anti-socialist stand the Fascists received strong support from the army and the Catholic Church. The Pope, Pius XI, had experienced the fear of communism while a papal representative in Poland in 1920. With a weak liberal government he was willing to give tacit support to the Fascists.

In October 1922 when the Fascists had a 'march on Rome' to gain power, King Victor Emmanuel III refused to send the army against them. Mussolini, the fascist leader, was appointed Prime Minister in a coalition government with nationalists and conservatives.

(b) Mussolini was appointed Prime Minister of Italy for a variety of reasons.

Firstly, he was appointed by King Victor Emmanuel III because the king feared a civil war. By October 1922 Italy seemed to be descending into civil war between Fascists on one hand and socialists and communists on the other. The liberal governments of Prime Ministers Giolitti and Facta seemed to be incapable of dealing with the situation. Mussolini's March on Rome forced the King to chose between the Fascists and their opponents.

The King preferred to side with the Fascists because they were nationalists. Mussolini had denounced the peace treaties at the end of the war as the 'mutilated peace'. He aimed to make Italy a strong European power. Mussolini also wanted Italy to have strong, stable government. Perhaps the most attractive part of Mussolini's ideas was his anti-socialism. He portrayed himself as the only person to stand between Italy and chaos.

This view received support from Pope Pius XI and the Italian Catholic Church.

Mussolini was appointed Prime Minister under the Italian constitution, which meant the King could dismiss him. Mussolini was also head of a government in which the Fascists were in a minority. The other parties were the nationalists and conservatives. Both these groups thought they could use Mussolini's blackshirts to defeat the socialists and bring political and economic stability.

Q2 **(a)** When Mussolini was made Prime Minister in October 1922 he still faced a lot of opposition.

Mussolini was head of a government in which the Fascists were a minority. They shared power with the nationalists and conservatives. Within parliament Mussolini faced opposition from the liberal politicians who had formed the governments before October 1922.

Mussolini also had to face opposition from the Catholic Populari Party. This had been formed shortly after the First World War. As the vast majority of Italians were catholic, this party posed a potential threat.

The most significant threat to Mussolini after 1922 came from the socialists and communists. Even though Fascist squads raided socialist offices and intimidated socialist politicians they were still popular, in particular in the Po Valley area of northern Italy. The most important opponent of Mussolini in the national parliament was Matteotti, a socialist MP. He constantly criticised the Fascist infringement of human rights.

Even within the Fascist Party Mussolini faced challenges to his authority from local Fascist bosses known as 'Ras'. They ran their own parts of Italy without consulting Mussolini.

Mussolini was able to deal effectively with many of these problems. The liberal politicians remained disunited. In 1924 Fascist thugs murdered Matteotti.

(b) In 1925 Mussolini was able to form a dictatorship for a number of reasons.

Firstly, and most importantly, Fascist political ideas were anti-democratic. They believed in political stability through strong government. Mussolini saw himself as Il Duce ('The Leader') of the Italian people. Once he acquired political power he did not want to give it up. Once he had become prime minister, in October 1922, it was only a matter of time before he created a dictatorship.

Mussolini was aided greatly by the Acerbo Electoral Law of 1923. This allowed the largest political party in an election to gain two-thirds of the seats.

The murder of Matteotti, the socialist MP, in 1924 created a major scandal. Most other politicians left parliament in protest – known as the Aventine Succession. This left the Fascists in complete control of government and parliament.

Also, by 1925 Mussolini was able to gain full control of the Fascist Grand Council bringing local Ras leaders under his control.

Therefore, in 1925 Mussolini seemed to have gained complete control. However, it was still possible for the King to dismiss him as prime minister. Instead, Victor Emmanuel III was willing to allow Mussolini to act as a dictator because Mussolini had the backing of the senior members of the armed forces.

OCR Unit 3: 'Europe and the World 1919–1989'

Italy 1919–1939

(a) Mussolini was able to come to power in Italy for a variety of reasons.

The most important reason was the weakness and instability of Italian governments. The liberal politicians who dominated Italian politics failed to give the country strong government. In the period from the end of the First World War until 1919, Italy had four governments. None of them seemed capable of dealing with the economic problems of Italy or the rise in political unrest after the war.

The most pressing issue in Italy from 1918 was the rise of socialism and communism. Because of the number of strikes, 1919 was referred to as the 'Red Year'. Many businessmen and landowners feared the growth of left-wing ideas.

Mussolini's Fascists seemed to be the only group willing to stand up to the socialists. Fascist squads of blackshirts attacked socialist and trade union offices. The local and national political authorities seemed to be incapable of dealing with the rise of left-wing unrest. Businessmen and landowners turned instead to supporting the Fascists.

Fascists also received support because they were strongly nationalist. They denounced the peace treaties at the end of the war. They believed Italy should have been given more territory because they were one of the victorious Allied powers.

As a result of their strong nationalist views and anti-socialism, the Fascists were popular with the Army and the Catholic Church. Both these saw the Fascists as the only hope of providing strong government and preventing civil war.

To force the King to accept the Fascists as part of the government, Mussolini organised a march on Rome in October 1922. The King was forced to choose between the Fascists or face the possibility of civil war. To avoid conflict and to strengthen the government, the King invited Mussolini to be Prime Minister in a coalition government with nationalists and conservatives.

Therefore, the most important reason for the rise of Mussolini to power was the weakness in government, which he exploited.

(b) In many ways Mussolini did achieve a stable country between 1922 and 1939.

In the whole period Italy had one government and one prime minister. The dictatorship that Mussolini created by 1925 gave Italy a strong, stable government for the first time since unification.

The image of a strong, stable and prosperous government was sustained by the use of propaganda. Mussolini was portrayed as Il Duce, the leader of the Italian people. Grandiose projects were highlighted by the media as great Fascist achievements. These included draining the Pontine marshes near Rome, the renovation of Rome's ancient buildings and constructing roads. In addition, Mussolini and his government appeared as strong, dynamic leaders on newsreels, in school textbooks and in newspapers.

To ensure that no adverse publicity reached the Italian people, censorship was in place. In addition, the secret police (OVRA) arrested and imprisoned political opponents of the government.

In 1929 Mussolini signed the Lateran Treaties with the Pope. This created the Vatican City State as an independent state within Rome. This ended decades of conflict between the Italian government and the Catholic Church, thereby bringing stability.

However, although Italy might have been stable politically it was not particularly prosperous.

Attempts to increase grain production – the Battle for Grain – and to increase the population – the Battle for Births – were both failures. Italy remained a relatively poor country. This was most noticeable in the southern area known as the Mezzogiorno. Mussolini attempted to stabilise the Italian currency. Known as Quota 90, it over-valued the Italian lira and made imports very expensive.

Therefore, although Mussolini was successful in making Italy stable it did not become particularly prosperous.

AQA Unit 1 Alternative J: 'The Origins and Consolidation of Totalitarian Dictatorships 1918–1939'

(a) The 'critics of democracy' mentioned in the source refers to the Fascists, Socialists and Communists. These wanted to replace democracy with a dictatorship. The Fascists wanted a strong, nationalist government to defend Italian interests. The Socialists and Communists wanted a dictatorship to redistribute wealth to the working classes and peasants.

(b) A one-party state was established in Italy in the inter-war period mainly because democratic governments were weak and unstable. They failed to deal effectively with Italy's post-war problems. These include disillusionment with the peace settlement, the rise of socialism and communism, and economic depression.

The fear of socialism and communism forced many businessmen and landowners to look to a political party that was willing to use direct action methods to combat the left wing. The Fascist Party offered this alternative. Fascist blackshirt squads attacked socialist and trade union organisations at a time when the official authorities seemed incapable of action.

The Fascists were also popular because they were strong nationalists and in favour of making Italy a great European power.

As a result of their policies and actions the Fascists received support from the armed forces and the Catholic Church. So when Mussolini organised the March on Rome in October 1922, the King was forced to back down. To prevent a civil war he offered the post of Prime Minister to Mussolini.

Once in power, Mussolini was able to create a one-party state. In 1923 the Acerbo Electoral Law enabled the Fascists to gain two-thirds of the seats in parliament. This was after they had won the election aided by intimidation by the 'blackshirts'.

In 1924 the most ardent critic of the Fascists in parliament, the socialist MP Matteotti, was murdered by Fascist thugs. In protest, opposition MPs walked out of parliament in an episode known as the Aventine Succession. This left the Fascists with complete power over parliament and government.

Therefore, by 1925 Mussolini had established a one-party state mainly because opposition groups were weak and divided.

(c) The role of the individual leader was very important in the development of the Italian Fascist state.

The use of censorship and propaganda ensured that Mussolini was portrayed as Il Duce, the leader of the Italian people. He appeared in official publications and in the media as the man of destiny who was to lead Italy to the position of a major European state with a large colonial empire.

Mussolini was able to live up to the role of national leader because of his personal qualities as an orator and his strong personality. He seemed to personify the vigour and dynamism of the Italian Fascist state. When the Pontine Marshes were drained, Mussolini was deliberately photographed stripped to the waist aiding the workers.

Mussolini was a very effective political tactician. He forced the king to appoint him Prime Minister with the March on Rome in 1922. He passed the Acerbo Electoral Law in 1923, which gave the Fascists control of parliament. He was able to use the Matteotti Affair to establish a dictatorship by 1925.

However, although the role of the individual leader was important there were other factors which aided the development of a one-party state in Italy. The most important of these was the weakness and division amongst Mussolini's political opponents. Once he had established a dictatorship by 1925, Mussolini did not face a serious challenge to his position until Italy was invaded by the Allies in 1943.

In addition, what political opposition existed was dealt with effectively by the secret police, the OVRA. They arrested and imprisoned political opponents. Censorship and propaganda also helped to silence opposition or distract the Italian people away from the failures of the regime.

Finally, the aims and policies of Fascism ensured the continuation of a one-party state. Fascism was dictatorial and anti-democratic by nature. Once

the Fascist state was established, Mussolini and the Fascists were not going to give up political power.

Therefore, the most important reason was the role of the individual leader. However, this does not mean it was the only reason. Other important factors, such as the weakness of opposition, were also important.

9 Germany 1918–1933

How to score full marks

Edexcel Unit 1: 'The Seeds of Evil: The Rise of National Socialism in Germany to 1933'

(a) Source 1 reveals that Goebbels was optimistic in May 1932 because President Hindenburg had lifted the ban on the Stormtroopers (SA). The SA were also allowed to wear their uniforms again. However, the main cause of optimism was the calling of a Reichstag election because of the resignation of Chancellor Bruning. Goebbels believed the Nazis would greatly increase their share of the vote. The Nazis would be able to use the SA to intimidate the opposition. Also, the government of Bruning had begun to crumble, according to Goebbels. This meant the Nazis would be able to win votes at their expense.

(b) The SA's role was to act as the paramilitary wing of the Nazi Party. From 1930 normal political activity was difficult in Germany because of the economic and political crisis. All major parties had paramilitary units. For instance, the Communists had the Red Front. The main role of the SA was to defend Nazi political meetings and to disrupt opponents' meetings.

The SA were important because they were the most effective paramilitary force in Germany between 1930 and January 1933. They helped disrupt the opposition very effectively. So much so that President Hindenburg banned them in early 1932. The SA were also a major method of recruitment of young men into the ranks of the Nazi Party. Many were unemployed and they were attracted by the uniform, regular wage and the opportunity for action. It is difficult to imagine the Nazi Party becoming so powerful before January 1933 without the support of the SA.

(c) Source 4 supports the views in Source 5 on Nazi support to a limited extent.

Firstly, it shows that across Germany the Nazis gained support. This supports the view in Source 5 that Nazi support was a 'mile wide'.

Secondly, the information in Source 4 suggests that the Nazis attracted support from different social groups and town and country. It shows that the Nazis attracted support in rural areas such as East Prussia and industrialised areas such as Dusseldorf.

However, Source 4 shows that the Nazis did not attract much support in Lower Bavaria, Berlin or Cologne-Aachen. This supports Source 5 when that source suggests Nazi support in places was an 'inch deep'.

Yet Source 4 does not refer to all the regions of Germany.

Therefore, Source 4 does, to a large extent, support the views expressed in Source 5.

(d) Both sources are of value to a historian studying the funding of the Nazis but in different ways.

Source 2 provides considerable factual information about the mechanics of fundraising. As it comes from the Nazi propaganda department it is an instruction to Nazi supporters of how to get the most money from meetings. However, it was written in 1931 and has limited value on fundraising at other periods.

Source 3 is an anti-Nazi poster and therefore is biased against the Nazis. It is trying to give the message to the general public that the Nazis are financed by Big Business. It is useful to a historian because it shows the type of anti-Nazi poster used in Germany in 1932. However, one should question its reliability because it is election propaganda.

(e) Traditional elites were an important factor in the rise of Hitler to power.

As stated in Source 1, President Hindenburg aided the rise of the Nazis in May 1932 by dismissing Chancellor Bruning and calling a Reichstag election. He also aided them by lifting the ban on the SA. As a result, the Nazis gained their best election result, gaining 230 seats in the Reichstag and becoming Germany's largest political party.

In the November 1932 Reichstag election Nazi support fell and they only achieved 196 seats. When Nazi support was falling, Hindenburg supported by other right-wing politicians offered Hitler the Chancellorship of Germany in January 1933.

However, the rise of Hitler cannot be understood without recognising the importance of other factors. As stated in Source 5, Nazi support was wide. The Nazis were able to play on dissatisfaction, resentment and fear. The Nazis were anti-communist. They were also against the Versailles settlement and offered radical solutions to the problems of unemployment.

In addition, the Nazis were led by a dynamic leader, Adolf Hitler, who was an excellent orator. Hitler's skills were effectively exploited by the Nazi propaganda department under Goebbels.

Also, opposition to the Nazis was weak and divided. The left wing was split between socialists and communists. The leaders of the nationalists and conservatives were also weak.

Therefore, the rise to power of Hitler was due to a variety of reasons. The most important was the severe economic depression faced by Germany from 1939, which brought a virtual collapse to the economic and political structure of Weimar Germany.

AQA Unit 1 Alternative G: 'Imperial and Weimar Germany 1866–1925'

(a) The 'existing internal conflict' which affected Germany in early 1919 were left-wing attempts to establish socialist and communist governments. The most serious attempt came in January 1919 when the Spartacist League, led by Rosa Luxembourg and Karl Liebknecht, attempted to create a communist-style government in Berlin. This led to an armed confrontation with right-wing militia known as Freikorps.

Also, in early 1919, Kurt Eisner formed a socialist republic in Bavaria based on the capital Munich. This also led to military conflict with the Freikorps.

(b) The Treaty of Versailles provoked outrage in Germany for a number of reasons.

The most important reason was Article 231, the War Guilt Clause. This claimed that Germany was solely responsible for starting the First World War. Most Germans believed they had fought a defensive war. Associated with War Guilt was Article 232, which forced Germany to pay huge reparations payments to the Allies.

In addition, Germany was forced to lose approximately 10% of its territory. By giving the Polish corridor to Poland, Germany was split in two with East Prussia as a separate area. Germany also lost its entire overseas empire.

Finally, Germany was forced to disarm. It lost its entire navy and its army was reduced to 100,000 men. This was smaller than the Danish army. In addition, the Rhineland was demilitarised and Germany was forced to accept an Allied army of occupation there.

(c) Right-wing opposition did cause many problems for the Weimar Republic up to 1925.

The most serious right-wing problem occurred in March 1920, called the Kapp Putsch. Right-wing Freikorps overthrew the government and supported an alternative right-wing government under Wolfgang Kapp. If the trade unions had not gone on general strike the Weimar Republic would have collapsed.

In addition, in the period up to 1922 right-wing assassination squads murdered leading Weimar politicians such as Mathias Erzberger and Walter Rathenau, the foreign minister.

Finally, in November 1923, Hitler and the Nazis created problems with the Beer Hall putsch in Munich. This was subdued relatively easily.

However, the Weimar Republic faced other serious difficulties. In 1919 socialists and communists tried to overthrow the Weimar government in Berlin and Munich. Without the support of the right-wing Freikorps the Republic could have collapsed.

Of greater importance were the economic problems associated with reparations and hyper-inflation in 1922–24. Hyper-inflation nearly brought about the collapse of the economy. It was caused initially by the government printing too much money in order to pay off reparations. It was made worse by the Franco–Belgian occupation of the Ruhr in 1923–24. By the end of 1923, the Weimar Republic faced economic and political collapse. Without the Dawes Plan it is difficult to see how the Weimar Republic could have survived.

Although right-wing opposition created serious problems it was not the main cause of difficulty faced by the Republic to 1925.

OCR Unit 3: 'European and World History 1789–1989'

Europe 1890–1945: 4 Germany 1919–1945

(a) The economic problems facing the Weimar Republic were very serious. They almost brought the collapse of the Republic between 1918 and 1924. They were the main reason for the rise of Hitler to power in 1933.

Between 1918 and 1924 economic problems were associated with the impact of the war and the Versailles settlement on Germany. These caused unemployment and economic hardship at first. By 1922 the attempt to pay reparations through printing money helped cause hyper-inflation. This was made worse by the Franco–Belgian occupation of the Ruhr industrial areas in 1923–24. These economic problems were so severe that the German currency, the Reichmark, all but lost its value. Only with US help was the currency stabilised in 1924 through the Dawes Plan.

By far the most serious economic difficulty was the economic depression from 1929. This was associated with mass unemployment and falling prices. This crisis was so severe it led directly to the rise in popularity of extremist political parties such as the Nazis and Communists. The depression created a major economic and political crisis from which the Weimar Republic did not recover. Democratic politicians seemed powerless to deal with its effects. Instead the President turned to Hitler to form a government in January 1933. This hastened the end of the Weimar Republic.

(b) The Nazi Party grew in popularity for a number of reasons.

The main reason was the economic depression, which caused mass unemployment in Germany after 1929. The extreme economic crisis led to the rise in popularity of political parties with extreme solutions to the problem. The Communists rose in popularity. However, the main benefactors were the Nazis who became the largest political party in Germany by May 1932.

Linked to the rise of the Nazis was fear of communism. The Nazis were seen by many as the only real opponents of the Communists. Democratic politicians were seen as weak and incapable of dealing with the economic depression.

The Nazis were also fortunate to gain support from traditional elites. These included the advisers of President Hindenburg. Using his constitutional powers, the President hired and fired all chancellors from 1930. He was the person who appointed Hitler as Chancellor in 1933.

Finally, the Nazis grew in popularity because they were led by a dynamic leader, Adolf Hitler, whose nationalist anti-communist and anti-democratic policies were popular with many Germans who had lost faith with the Weimar Republic.

10 The Cold War

How to score full marks

AQA Unit 1 Alternative L: 'US Foreign Policy 1890–1991'

(a) The Truman Doctrine of April 1947 introduced the policy of containment. The aim of this policy was, literally, to contain the growth of communism – firstly in Europe, and, later, around the world. Truman introduced the policy in the Spring of 1947 following the British announcement that due to financial reasons it could no longer help in the defence of Greece and Turkey.

(b) Truman was very successful in his handling of the Soviet blockade of Berlin in 1948–49.

When faced with the Soviet blockade of all land routes between the western Allied zones of occupation and west Berlin, Truman had a number of options. He could have abandoned west Berlin to possible Soviet rule. This would have been a major blow to his policy of containment. Alternatively, Truman could have used armed force to free the routes to west Berlin. This could have resulted in a major war between the USA and USSR.

Instead, Truman chose to supply west Berlin from the air. This involved round-the-clock flights using British and American aircraft.

Truman was very successful because the Soviets lifted their blockade in 1949. It was a triumph for containment. It also helped Truman in the creation of the North Atlantic Treaty Organisation (NATO) as the main defence for western Europe against possible Soviet aggression.

(c) In many ways Truman's Administration was successful in its relations with the USSR in Europe between 1945 and 1949.

Firstly, in the Truman Doctrine, the United States successfully defended Greece and Turkey against possible communist influence. In Greece, the communists were defeated in the civil war. In Turkey, Soviet attempts to influence the country were halted.

In the Marshall Plan of 1947 the USA helped to prevent the growth of communism through economic aid. Between 1947 and 1952, $13 billion was used to help western Europe recover from the Second World War. As a result, communist threats to countries such as France and Italy receded.

The most successful achievement of US policy was in Germany. In 1948–49 the Americans defeated the Berlin Blockade. The following year, the three western zones of occupation were

united to form the Federal Republic of Germany. Backed by the forces of NATO, central Europe was able to provide an effective barrier to possible Soviet aggression.

However, Truman was not always successful. His abrasive manner helped bring a rapid deterioration in US–Soviet relations from April 1945. The military confrontation in Europe was partly his fault.

The climate of distrust created by Truman divided Europe into two opposing camps: one communist; the other non-communist. By 1947, all Soviet-liberated Europe had become communist except for Czechoslovakia.

The loss of Czechoslovakia to communist control in the Spring of 1948 was the major failure of US policy in Europe between 1845 and 1949.

Perhaps, the biggest blow to Truman's relations with the USSR came with the successful testing of a Soviet atomic bomb in 1949. This forced Europe into the agreement of nuclear warfare between the two superpowers.

Therefore, I would agree that, on balance, Truman was quite successful in his dealing with the USSR in Europe up to 1949.

OCR Unit 3: 'Europe and the World 1919–1989'

3 The Cold War in Europe 1945–1989

(a) The collapse of the Grand Alliance against Nazi Germany occurred for a number of reasons.

The most important reason was the ideological conflict between the USA and Britain, on one hand, and the USSR on the other. The western Allies were in favour of capitalism and democracy; the USSR was in favour of communism. In many ways the Alliance of 1941–45 was an interlude in the conflict between these two sides which had begun with the Bolshevik Revolution of 1917.

Suspicions between the two sides were apparent at the Yalta and Potsdam conferences which occurred in 1945. Neither side could agree on a formal peace treaty to end the war. Instead, the suspicions and feeling of distrust were important in breaking up the Grand Alliance. This was made worse when the USA dropped atomic bombs on Japan in August 1945.

Also important was the Soviet takeover of much of eastern Europe between 1945 and 1947. Virtually all the states 'liberated' by the Red Army were forced to have communist governments. So concerned were the western

Allies that Churchill's 'Iron Curtain' speech of 1946 was seen as the western view of Soviet action.

However, part of the blame must rest with President Truman. His abrasive style of dealing with Soviet politicians, such as foreign minister Molotov, created tension between the superpowers. Soviet fears about Truman were made worse with the launch of the Truman Doctrine in 1947, in which Truman planned to contain the growth of communism in Europe.

Therefore, it would seem that the collapse of the Grand Alliance was inevitable once the war against Germany and Japan had come to an end.

(b) The Soviet Union used a variety of methods to maintain control over eastern Europe between 1945 and 1989.

The most important method was the use of the Red Army. Eastern Europe was effectively occupied by Soviet armed forces over the whole period. This prevented individual states from trying to remove Soviet influence. The Red Army was used successfully to defeat anti-communist forces in the Berlin Uprising of 1953, the Hungarian Uprising of 1956 and the Prague Spring in Czechoslovakia in August 1968.

Another important method was to close the borders between communist eastern Europe and the West. The development of the Iron Curtain prevented people leaving for the West. It also prevented western propaganda infiltrating the Soviet occupied part of Europe. The last part of the Iron Curtain to be completed was the Berlin Wall in 1961. This method was quite successful because it did limit western influence. However, it did not stop it completely. Radio stations such as Radio Free Europe and later western television could be picked up in the Eastern Bloc. This helped undermine Soviet control.

Another method was to install communist governments in all the Eastern Bloc countries. These national communist parties were all answerable to the communist leadership in the USSR. This ensured strong political control.

Economic control was aided by the creation of Comecon, an Eastern Bloc equivalent of the European Union. The difference was that the USSR dominated it. All Eastern Bloc countries were forced to join and forced to trade with the USSR.

Finally, control was maintained through the use of propaganda and education. All states were forced to indoctrinate their populations in the benefits of the communist way of life. Political dissidents were arrested and imprisoned by the political police of each state. This occurred in Poland in 1981–82, when the Solidarity trade union was suppressed by the Polish police and armed forces.

Therefore, Soviet control was generally successful. No state had left the communist fold until 1989.

4 The Cold War in Asia and the Americas 1949–1975

(a) The Cuban Missile Crisis of October 1962 was a very serious threat to international peace.

It occurred at a delicate period of the Cold War. The young US President, John F. Kennedy, had suffered serious defeats in his foreign policy. In 1961 a humiliating defeat of anti-Castro forces had occurred in the Bay of Pigs invasion. In August 1961 the eastern Germans had built the Berlin Wall. By the time Soviet nuclear missiles were discovered on Cuba, only 90 miles from the USA, it was clear a major crisis would occur.

The problem was made worse because Soviet leader Khrushchev completely underestimated President Kennedy's ability to offer stern resistance to the Soviet move.

As a result of these developments, it was clear a major crisis would occur.

It was a major threat to international peace because both superpowers had already placed their armed forces on a war footing. In addition, both based their defence on the use of nuclear weapons that had the destructive power to destroy the earth.

The decision by Kennedy to quarantine the island of Cuba therefore created an acute crisis just short of all-out nuclear war.

The immediate aftermath of the crisis also reflected its importance. Both sides signed a nuclear test ban treaty in 1963. They also opened up the Molink, a direct telephone line between the White House and the Kremlin.

(b) Three factors which contributed to the failure of the USA to win the Vietnam War were the use of guerrilla tactics by the communists, the opposition to the war in the USA and the ineffective tactics used by the US armed forces.

The use of guerrilla tactics was very effective. The communists used these tactics effectively in the jungle and mountainous terrain of Vietnam to engage in hit-and-run tactics against the American and South Vietnamese forces. It proved very difficult to locate and destroy communist forces. It also led to a major drop in morale in US forces following the communist Tet Offensive of 1968.

These guerrilla tactics showed up the shortcomings of US military search-and-destroy tactics. These were started by General

Westmoreland. They failed to pin down and defeat the communists. As a result, the Americans and South Vietnamese controlled some territory during the day, only for the communists to take control at night. The hoped-for major military confrontation between the US forces and the communists never occurred.

This led the USA to adopt more drastic tactics: blanket bombing, the use of napalm and the use of defoliants had a devastating effect on the Vietnamese landscape. Frustration at not being able to defeat the communists led to atrocities, such as the My Lai massacre of 1968.

The failure of the United States to score a decisive victory, the controversial US military tactics and the rising casualty rate all had an adverse effect on opinion within the USA. From the Tet Offensive in 1968 a major anti-war movement developed. This forced President Johnson not to run for a second term as president in 1968. It eventually forced President Nixon to reduce troop levels and try to negotiate a way out of the war from 1969.

Each of these factors combined to force the USA to abandon its military commitment to the Vietnam conflict from 1969. Once the United States began to withdraw its armed forces, it was a matter of time before the communists would be victorious in the war.